Skills for Group Practice
Responding to Diversity

Skills for Group Practice
Responding to Diversity

Stephen Erich

University of Houston – Clear Lake

Heather Kanenberg

University of Houston – Clear Lake

Allyn & Bacon

Boston Columbus Indianapolis New York San Francisco Upper Saddle River
Amsterdam Cape Town Dubai London Madrid Milan Munich Paris Montreal Toronto
Delhi Mexico City Sao Paulo Sydney Hong Kong Seoul Singapore Taipei Tokyo

Executive Editor: *Ashley Dodge*
Editorial Assistant: *Carly Czech*
Senior Marketing Manager: *Wendy Albert*
Marketing Assistant: *Kyle VanNatter*
Production Assistant: *Maggie Brobeck*
Manufacturing Buyer: *Debbie Rossi*
Cover Administrator: *Kristina Mose-Libon*
Editorial Production and Composition Service: *Alliance Publishing*
Interior Design: *Alliance Publishing*

10 9 8 7 6 5 4 3 2 1   14 13 12 11 10

Allyn & Bacon
is an imprint of

www.pearsonhighered.com

ISBN 10: 0-205-61005-6
ISBN 13: 978-0-205-61005-1

CONTENTS

Angela

A NOTE TO THE INSTRUCTOR

This text is a skills book of role play exercises for treatment and task groups that emphasizes diversity (including sex, sexual orientation, gender identity/expression, race, ethnic background, language, national origin, religion, marital status, class, health status, mental or physical ability, age, socio-economic status, and political belief) and the experience of group facilitation. The exercises in this skills book provide BSW & MSW students with wonderful opportunities to engage in "real life" group experiences, or at least a close approximation of working with real clients. The book is structured with a brief introduction to group theories and skills to serve as a reminder to students of the knowledge and skills they have learned in their coursework. Topic areas for the exercises include 1) treatment groups, such as support groups, social skills groups, educational groups, growth groups, and therapy groups; and 2) task groups, such as interdisciplinary teams, coalitions, grant writing teams and political action committees (PAC). The exercises include open groups and the beginning, middle, and end stage of closed groups. The content on issues related to diversity is designed to prepare students for work in our multicultural global community.

A core group of these exercises have been researched, implemented, and evaluated in the classroom over a period of five years. While initially there certainly were doubts about how well these types of activities would work in the classroom setting, these were quickly set aside. Students and alumni from our BSW Program have rated the value of their "group work" experiences very highly. Formal student feedback from the Baccalaureate Education Assessment Program (BEAP) suggests students believe they have a "very good" to "excellent" understanding of group work issues. Field Instructors and employers have indicated that students in our program display solid foundational skills in group work practice. Lastly, anecdotal feedback from our alumni typically include comments like the following, "these group experiences really helped to prepare me for facilitating groups with real clients," and "I learned so much from this [group] class".

ESSENTIAL ELEMENTS OF THE EXERCISES

We want to start by telling you that we hope you will review what we've provided here and recognize that it can and should be modified to best meet your needs, the educational needs of students, and the goals of the classroom. We have provided throughout the text some options for you, but we strongly encourage you to make meaning of the exercises and content in a way that will advance the knowledge, skills, and values of your students in their pursuit of professional social work careers. Additionally, we recognize that because our institutions and social work programs have varied curricula, course schedules, semester/trimester lengths, and so on, there will likely be some adjustments that might lead to a better "fit" of this text with your course. It is our sincerest hope that this text will serve as a resource and opportunity for you and your students!

Each of the exercises typically involves seven to twelve students. One or two students are selected to facilitate the designated group for a portion of the class period or lab. Student group facilitators are to be given specific instructions to assist them with each stage of facilitating the group. Most student group members will participate in discussions involving typical behavior that may be expected in any of the sample group scenarios. One or two of the students from this group will be designated as the Jokers. The term "Joker" is used here to refer to students playing the role of a confederate—that is, she/he is acting out a predefined role for a given exercise. We consciously selected the term Joker over other options because it seems to carry the least "baggage" and be the most accessible to students. The Jokers receive specific, unique, and confidential instructions from you that involve them engaging in a specific set of behaviors, in part designed to create a dynamic group experience while also providing a real life opportunity to practice important group skills. The remaining students in the class are "observers-only" during the group process. However, it is expected that observers are actively involved in post-group discussion.

At the end of each designated group, all students participate in a post-group exercise. This process typically begins with the student group facilitators describing their experience leading the group. They are expected to share their thoughts and emotions experienced during the group and provide a critique of their work that includes a specific and balanced assessment of their strengths and areas for improvement. Then each actively participating group member, including the Jokers, shares her/his thoughts and emotions experienced during the group and provide specific and balanced feedback for the facilitators. The final portion of the activity involves all members of the class, including observers, discussing the entire group activity.

WHY YOU NEED THE ACCOMPANYING INSTRUCTOR'S MANUAL

There are more important tips for using this skills book in the Instructor's Manual including how to help students prepare and facilitate the practice groups, as well as some more suggestions of how to use this skills book in your Group Practice course. **Additionally, it will be essential that you use this instructor's manual as you work with each student group engaging in an exercise.** You will be helping the (co)facilitators prepare for their role, you will be helping the group members get centered, and you will be assigning the **Joker** roles to one or more students. Doing these things will help make the exercises all that they can be and will result in a rich learning experience for all members of your classroom! To that end, in each chapter of the instructors manual we highlight important preparation points, **Joker** roles, optional homework activities, and more, in large off-set boxes. They are easy to find throughout the chapter and should provide you with both necessary material for a successful preparation of students, and also an opportunity to be creative and alter the experience as you like.

So, please keep an eye out for these boxes and remember that the exercises will not live up to their potential without the Joker role (or a Joker role) being assigned!

To access the Instructor's Manual, visit Pearson's Instructor Resource Center at: www.pearsonhighered.com. Search ISBN: 0-205-61008-0. Or to contact your local Pearson sales representative at www.pearsonhighered.com/replocator.

ACKNOWLEDGEMENTS

Arch would like to thank Livia, Josh, and Nicki for making him the luckiest guy in the world.

Heather would like to thank Matthew — your love and patience are amazing and help sustain me. Mad Love to Mom, Dad, Liz, Dave, Scott, Lynda and James: you are the world's best family! I dedicate this book to Cheryl Wayne Sweet — you'll never know how much I thank you for instilling an appreciation of all diversity in me.

Together we thank Terri Culbert for her unending support; Carly Czech for her guidance; Patricia Quinlin for her support in getting this project off the ground; and Ashley Dodge for taking over in a pinch. We share great appreciation for our colleague's contributions and innovative work. It has been an exciting opportunity to co-author several of the exercises in this text with students from our BSW program. Collectively, the contributions of all the authors have helped to enrich the professional development of Social Work students, and for this we thank you! Last, but not least, we'd like express our sincere appreciation to "Student Worker Extraordinaire": Ty David Lerman, for his diligent work in supporting the project from beginning to end.

CONTRIBUTOR NOTES

Stephen "Arch" Erich, Ph.D., LCSW is currently an Associate Professor and the Program Director of the Bachelor of Social Work program at the University of Houston- Clear Lake. His research, practice, and advocacy interests are subsumed under the umbrella of strengthening diverse family structures. With over 28 years of social work experience, Dr. Erich has worked with many different types of families, including those who have children with autism, as well as families experiencing other developmental challenges. He also spent a number of years working with families who had adopted children with special needs. Dr. Erich has published numerous scholarly articles. His research and advocacy have centered on two primary themes: adoptive families; especially those with lesbian and gay parents and transgender persons and their families. Dr. Erich has served as a consulting editor and reviewer for several academic journals and most recently served as the Guest Editor for a special issue of the journal *Adoption Quarterly* dedicated to the topic of "Gay and Lesbian Issues in Adoption."

Heather Kanenberg, Ph.D., LMSW is currently the Director of Field Education and Assistant Professor with the University of Houston-Clear Lake Bachelor of Social Work Program.   Dr. Kanenberg also serves as an active member of the Women's Studies Faculty at UHCL. She obtained her BSW from Murray State University and her MSW and Ph.D. from the University of Houston. Dr. Kanenberg has taught at the graduate and undergraduate level for 8 years, her teaching includes courses such as: Women's Issues, Ethics, Introduction to Social Work, Policy Analysis, and Field Seminar. Throughout her career as a professional social worker she has worked as an advocate on behalf of many oppressed and disenfranchised populations, with a primary focus on Children's Health, Women's Health, and Public Policy. Examples of her professional experiences include working with county health departments and as a public policy analyst, and experience working with advocacy organizations. Dr. Kanenberg's research agenda includes a focus on feminist policy analysis and frameworks. She is concerned with underrepresented populations, and issues such as access to healthcare for women and girls, adoptive families with gay and lesbian parents, and issues specific to the transgender community.

CONTRIBUTORS

Sharon K. Hall, Ph.D. is Associate Professor of Psychology at the University of Houston, Clear Lake. She is a member of the Association for Psychological Science, the American Psychological Association and the American Association of University Women. Her current research interests are in trauma and resilience, as well as in obesity prevention in children. She has published numerous articles on developmental psychology, as well as a critically acclaimed book, *Raising Kids in the 21st Century: The Science of Psychological Health for Children in 2008.*

Rhonda Harvey, BSW obtained her BSW in May 2009, from the University of Houston, Clear Lake. In fall 2009, she is currently enrolled in graduate studies as a recipient of a Hartford Fellowship, concentrating on the area of gerontology at the University of Houston's Graduate College of Social Work.

Sandra A. Lopez is a Licensed Clinical Social Worker with twenty nine years of social work practice experience. She holds the distinctions of Academy Certified Social Worker and Diplomat in Clinical Social Work through the National Association of Social Workers. Since her graduation from the University of Houston's Graduate School of Social Work in 1980, she has worked in a variety of settings, including hospital, family service agency, private practice, and academia. Ms. Lopez presently serves as Clinical Associate Professor at the University of Houston – Graduate College of Social Work, where she primarily teaches courses related to clinical practice. She is recognized for her established expertise in the field of traumatic grief. She has held various leadership positions within NASW since her graduation from her master's program to the present. Currently, she has devoted her professional work to the importance of professional self-care for social workers and other helping professionals. She has to date trained thousands of professionals on the natural consequences of helping stress, burnout, compassion fatigue and secondary trauma.

Susan Mapp, Ph.D., MSSW, is Associate Professor and Chair of the Department of Social Work, Elizabethtown College. She is the author of two books on issues in international social work and has presented her research at numerous national and international conferences.

Mary Ann Nguyen, BSW graduated from the University of Houston at Clear Lake in May 2009 with a bachelor's degree in social work, and is currently pursuing a master's degree in social work at the University of Houston's Graduate College of Social Work. Mary Ann is a member of the Iroquois tribe (Six Nations of the Grand River) and is interested in working with Native American and other minority and oppressed populations, with an emphasis on social justice and reducing disparities in the field of healthcare.

Yvonne Okonkwo, is a student in the UHCL BSW program and will graduate in spring 2011. Her areas of interest are policy analysis, international affairs, and urban development. Her professional aspirations are to improve the lives of vulnerable, misrepresented, and abused children, including AIDS orphans in Africa, street children in Brazil, and at-risk youth/teens in the U.S. Her future goal is to create policy initiatives that advance social equality with a focus on researching empirically verifiable applications and approaches required to modify pathologic social conditions and policies that further economic inequality, judicial injustices, health disparity, and racial/gender discriminatory practices.

Amy Russell earned her MSW and Ph.D. in Social Work from the University of Houston. Dr. Russell has ten year's practice experience in public community mental health services working with persons with severe and persistent mental illness. Currently, tenure-track faculty at Texas State University, she has taught a variety of graduate and undergraduate level courses including: research methods, policy courses, ethics, advocacy research, behavioral statistics, and individual and group social work practice. Her research interests comprise cultural oppression and liberated identity, lesbian feminism, social capital, social welfare policy and economics, and lesbian and women's health and mental health needs. This agenda includes a special interest in research methods that utilize creative methods and classic grounded theory. Dr. Russell is politically active at the state-level and frequently presents on lobbying and advocacy ethics.

Kay Schiller is a Licensed Clinical Social Worker through the Texas State Board of Social Worker Examiners. Ms. Schiller has over eighteen years of practice experience as a Social Worker. She also holds the distinctions of Academy Certified Social Worker and Diplomat in Clinical Social Work through the National Association of Social Workers. Since her graduation from the University of Houston Graduate School of Social Work in 1989, she has worked in a variety of settings, including psychiatric hospital/professional practice, partial hospitalization, FEMA disaster counseling, private practice, and as an adjunct in academia for the University of Houston Graduate College of Social Work, University of Houston-Clear Lake, and Stephen F. Austin University as a field liaison. She is currently in private practice, teaches as an adjunct at both the University of Houston Graduate College of Social Work and the University of Houston – Clear Lake, and provides supervision for licensure and consultation. For the past 10 years, she has provided clinical supervision for social workers in a variety of settings including hospice, family service, mental health, schools, women's centers, and family violence unit for court services.

Marilyn T. Scott is currently a student at UHCL, working towards a Bachelors degree in Social Work, with a proposed graduation date of May 2010. She has volunteered as a child care worker at the Bay Area Turning Point Women and Children's Shelter since January 2007. Her areas of interest include foster and adoptive care for children, as well as improving the systems in which these children are placed.

Erin Sivil, BSW graduated from the University of Houston- Clear Lake in 2009 with a bachelor's degree in social work. She is currently continuing her education at the University of Houston by pursuing a master's degree in social work. Upon graduating, she hopes to work directly with individuals with substance abuse and mental health disorders. Erin is also interested in influencing policies that impact direct services for these populations. She spends most of her free time with her boyfriend and family, and enjoys camping and hiking in the Texas hill country.

Julie Underwood is currently a student at the University of Houston Clear Lake and anticipates graduating with a Bachelors degree in Social Work in the spring of 2010. After earning her BSW, she plans to continue her education toward an MSW in a social work program that specializes in macro practices, including political social work, advocacy, and community organizing. With her social work education, she plans to conduct research and advocate for those who have serious mental illnesses.

Nicole Willis, LMSW has 10 years of experience working in the areas of mental health, education, and school social work. She has experience teaching and co-teaching courses in research, introduction to social work, grief and bereavement as well as various courses in HBSE in both BSW and MSW programs. Nicole is currently working on her PhD in social work (ABD), and has research interests in the fields of adolescent resilience, parental incarceration, and child welfare program evaluation. Currently, Nicole practices as a bilingual school social worker, is adjunct faculty, and serves on several committees in the community.

SECTION 1

USING THE TEXT

CHAPTER 1

INTRODUCTION & WHAT TO EXPECT

Congratulations! You are at the point in your professional social work education where you are focusing on the development and building of skills for direct practice. Specifically, you are working to advance your skills of group (co)facilitation. As we will soon explain, this text is designed to be used along with your text, but it is important that you understand the structure of what we're giving you and how it can be a valuable resource for you. Within this text you'll find many exercises that are opportunities for you (or you and a classmate) to role-play with your peers and facilitate a group session. We've worked with the contributors to ensure that these scenarios, in total, represent a significant amount of diversity in terms of population, nature of the group, purpose of the group, and other additional factors. The goal is to give you and your peers an opportunity to practice your skills and hone your craft as professional social workers as you prepare for the exercises, engage with them, reflect on the experience, and self-assess after the role play. In addition, these exercises afford your instructor an opportunity to observe your preparation process, utilization of skills, and capacity to self-assess. This presents a unique learning opportunity whereby your instructor can give you very specific individualized feedback. It also creates an environment for you to learn from the strengths and weaknesses of your peers. So, what have we provided for you here?

THE CHAPTERS: DECONSTRUCTED

Each chapter includes a single group session scenario that students will (co)facilitate. In these scenarios, some of your peers will serve as group members and other students will serve as observers. Included in each exercise is an introduction to the group, a brief amount of context for the scenario, prompts, theories, and skills that are related and useful when considering (co)facilitating the group. There is a description of the group itself, the group membership generally present, the stage of group development (when appropriate), as well as key concepts and principles for (co)facilitators to consider while reflecting on that specific exercise. At the end of each chapter is a listing of web-based resources that will facilitate your understanding of issues related to the exercise (e.g., population of interest, services, helping models, etc.). Your text also includes a bibliography that has scholarly resources organized by chapter to assist with your preparation as a group facilitator.

Your instructor will talk with you, but it is expected that you'll do research into the area of service delivery that your specific scenario covers as you prepare for your turn to (co)facilitate. There are resources provided (both scholarly academic work in the bibliography of the text and information from the web at the end of each chapter) for you to begin this research. However, we caution you not to consider the resources we've provided as the only resources available. It will be particularly important that you research local information that is relevant to your community!

The Joker(s)

One more important piece of information for you about the chapters: each exercise has a "joker" role or two that one or more of your classmates will play in the groups! Yes, your instructor has the associated instructor's manual for the text, which has joker roles identified for each exercise in the text. This will result in her/him pulling aside one or more members of the group and assigning them a task, position, or issue to act out during the exercise. The idea is to give you an opportunity to really "think on your feet" and to practice what it's like in the field when groups don't go as smoothly as planned. Naturally, this "unknown" will cause you anxiety, but it also should serve as a challenge to you to make sure you're ready with all your knowledge and skills and prepared to respond when the "joker" surfaces.

If you are role playing as a "group member" instead of as a co-facilitator, you will need to develop your character for that specific group session. This should be done with your instructor and the other students who are role playing for that particular group so that characters do not duplicate one another. When developing your character, we strongly encourage you and your role playing classmates to ensure that the group is composed of a diverse array of individuals, including those from oppressed or marginalized groups.

Reflection/Process Prompts

A key element of your participation in these exercises is your capacity to critique your peers (if you are a participant or observer in the group) or to self-assess (if you are the (co)facilitator). We've provided you with prompts for the post-group reflection activity to be completed after each in-class exercise. The reflection and processing is to happen immediately after the group experience, and is designed so that all members of the class (participants, observers, co-facilitators, and jokers) will engage in the balanced assessment. The goal of this post group exercise is to provide you an opportunity to do an assessment of the experience, to develop your skills of processing, and to provide feedback. No matter what role you take, ideally you will be able to provide a balanced, thorough critique of the experience that displays careful consideration of the exercise and the performance of the co-facilitators.

THEORY AND SKILL REVIEW

Included in this workbook you'll also find a review of many relevant theories, concepts, and skills to help inform your social work group practice. These bulleted lists and tables are designed to support and reinforce materials you have been provided previously (via lecture, textbooks, research, etc.). These should be considered one resource as you prepare to (co)facilitate your group and when you reflect on your experience after the exercise.

Theories

You are about to engage in experiential exercises that will advance your group skills, knowledge, and values. Undoubtedly, your instructor has provided you with a wealth of information on these constructs; you likely also have a textbook with theoretical content on group work practice. This information is most valuable as you initiate the role plays in this workbook. As one last opportunity to review the key concepts of group theory and practice, we've provided you the following bulleted list to reinforce your use of and access to such important information.

Influential Theories/Perspectives

- *Person in Environment Perspectives*: Our profession has adopted the theoretical perspective that to fully understand the human condition, we must understand the interaction between people and the environment, as well as cultural factors, including those related to equal access and power differences. In a related manner, social workers use the bio-psycho-social-spiritual perspective as a means for understanding human behavior across four key dimensions of human behavior. The following theories provide unique but related information that helps explain the behavior of groups and individuals in groups:

- *System theories* represent a type of Person in Environment Perspective. Systems theories attempt to understand the group as a system. A system is a set of elements that are interacting in an organized manner to make a functional whole (Kirst-Ashman & Hull, 2009). A system may take the form of an individual, family, group, organization, or community. Homeostasis refers to a systems natural tendency to strive for a relative state of balance, although not all "states of balance" are optimally healthy. All systems have boundaries that are to one degree or another porous, allowing the potential for exchanges of information, resources, and energy to move in and out of a system. Every system is also a subsystem of a larger system, or a supra system, to other subsystems. Systems act upon and react to their environments. As systems grow in size they become increasingly more complex with higher degrees of differentiation and specialization among the systems components. A cornerstone of systems thinking is *Equifinality*, which refers to the idea that there are often many different means to the same end, or in other words, there are many ways of understanding and solving a problem.

- *The Ecological Model* developed by Bronfenbrenner (1979) suggests there are four levels of the environment that interact simultaneously and reciprocally with individuals.

  1. The *Mircrosystem* includes children and parents and those in the immediate family environment.
  2. The *Mesosystem* includes teachers, employers, bosses, friends, and relatives who also have a direct and indirect influence on individuals.
  3. The *Exosystem* includes social institutions like local government, the community, schools, places of worship, local media, etc.
  4. The *Macrosystem* includes larger government institutions, educational systems, religious systems, political thought, and economic systems.

- *Ecological Perspective*: Carol Germaine was a pioneer of the Ecological Systems Theory (Germain, 1991). This perspective views people and environments as a unitary system within a particular cultural and historical context. Both person and environment can be fully understood only in terms of their relationship with one another. This perspective emphasizes a collaborative client-social worker relationship where the clients are the experts in their own lives. Empowerment results from successful social action carried out jointly by clients and social workers or by clients by themselves. Problems are viewed not as existing in the person only but in the total person-in-environment complex. The therapeutic goal is to improve the degree of "fit" between the person and various aspects of their environment. When the fit is generally positive, it represents a state of relative adaptedness that promotes continued development and satisfying social functioning and sustains or enhances the environment.

- In keeping with a *Systems Perspective*, Bales (1958) suggests that groups have two general types of problems to overcome:

    1. Instrumental problems, such as reaching group and individual goals, and
    2. Socio-emotional problems, which include interpersonal problems, problems of coordination and member satisfaction. The Bales model suggests that groups vacillate between adaptation to the outside environment and attention to internal integration.

- *Field Theory*: According to Field theory (Kurt Lewin, 1944), the group is best viewed as a "Gestalt," which is an evolving entity of opposing forces that act to hold members in the group and to move the group along in its quest for goal achievement. Lewin (1944) developed the following concepts:

    1. Roles   The status, rights, and duties of group members.
    2. Norms   The rules governing the behavior of group members.
    3. Power   The ability of members to influence one another.
    4. Cohesion   The amount of attraction the members of a group feel for one another and the group.
    5. Consensus   The degree of agreement regarding goals and other group phenomena.
    6. Valence   The potency of goals and objects in the life space of the group.

- *Structural Functionalism*, developed by Tallcot Parsons, defined groups as social systems with several different interdependent members attempting to maintain order and a stable equilibrium while they function as a unitary whole (Ashford, LeCroy, & Lortie, 2006). Parsons identified four functional (and essential) tasks of group systems (Ashford, LeCroy, & Lortie, 2006):

    1. Integration: ensuring that members of groups fit together.
    2. Adaptation: ensuring that groups change to cope with the demands of the environment.
    3. Pattern maintenance: ensuring that groups define and sustain their basic purposes, identities, and procedures.
    4. Goal attainment: ensuring that groups pursue and accomplish their tasks.

- *Feminist Theories*: Feminist theories have evolved over time with a goal of explaining the disenfranchisement of women. Several Feminist theories are now widely accepted as well-developed explanations of the oppression of all devalued groups (Gilligan, 1982; Friedan, 1975). A concept central to understanding Feminist theories is the idea of a "Patriarchy," which is the name given the current system of values, thoughts, laws, policies that favors men and in particular those men who are also White, Straight, Christian, and affluent (Hill

Collins, 2000). Characteristics of Feminist theories include avoiding labels, emphasizing current concerns, assessing environmental impact, assessing the devalued qualities of clients, evaluating current societal conditions, encouraging clients to uncover societal forces that prohibit productive changes, and encourage social action that will help promote public awareness toward existing problems (Hooks, 2000). It is important to note that there are many different feminist theories (Ex: Liberal, Radical, Social, etc.).

- *Queer Theory*: Postmodern Queer Theory argues that gender identity, gender roles and sexual orientation are not binary constructs, as most of the society views them, but rather fluid and dynamic, as most clearly manifested in the transgender community (Burge, 2007). Transgender, lesbian, and gay persons living outside the strict confines of the traditional binary construction of gender become vulnerable to discrimination in the form of harassment, social and familial rejection, workplace discrimination, denial of parental rights, and physical and sexual assault from those who abide by and enforce this narrow definition of gender and sexuality (Burdge, 2007; Erich, Tittsworth, & Kersten, in press; Roen, 2001).

- *The Strengths Perspective:* The Strengths Perspective (Saleebey, 2009) seeks out and amplifies client strengths which are then used to resolve client issues. Strengths may include cultural and behavioral variables, including the ability to find resources and collaborate with others. A primary goal is to empower clients to make necessary changes for themselves, to increase self-reliance and esteem, and to teach tools and skills for future needs.

- *The Empowerment Perspective*: The Empowerment Perspective (Gutierrez, DeLois, & GlenMaye, 1995) recognizes the effects of discrimination and oppression upon individual and group behavior and specifically seeks to assess powerlessness, group stigmatization, and devalued group membership. Likewise it is concerned with an analysis of economic, social and cultural forces among groups. It is also concerned with subjective and objective experiences with oppression and seeks to develop client power intrapersonally, interpersonally and politically.

- *Cognitive/Behavioral Theories*: Behavioral theories suggest people are basically shaped by their environments. The goal is to eliminate maladaptive behavior and learn constructive behavior. Behavioral theory as it relates to group work focuses primarily on the individual rather than the behavior of groups. Characteristics of practice include: clear and specific goal setting; contracting; the influence of the environment on the group and its members, step by step treatment planning, measurable treatment outcomes, and evaluation (Toseland & Rivas, 2009).

Cognitive theories are based on a client's pattern of thinking. According to these perspectives, our problems are caused by our perception or thoughts of life situations and not by the situations or past events themselves. The goal of the helping process is to eliminate unhealthy thinking while simultaneously developing new health-promoting ways of thinking (Toseland & Rivas, 2009).

According to Albert Bandura (1977) the behavior of group members can be explained by one of three methods of learning:

1. Classical Learning, or "conditioning," where a behavior becomes associated with a stimulus. Ex. The dog, bell, food, and salivating;

2. Operant Learning or "conditioning" where consequences after a given behavior determine the likelihood of that behavior continuing; or

3. Social Learning Theory which proposes that learning most often comes about as a result of observation and vicarious reinforcement or punishment. So when a group member is praised for something, the behavior is more likely to occur again for all members of the group.

- According to Psychodynamic theory, group members act out in the group un-resolved conflicts from early life experiences that are likely functioning in unconscious ways (Toseland & Rivas, 2009; Payne, 1997). In many ways, the group becomes a re-enactment of the family of origin situation (Toseland & Rivas, 2009).

According to Toseland and Rivas, (2009) Sigmund Freud originally described the group leader as a powerful father figure who has significant influence over other group members. Group members identify with the leader as the "ego ideal". Members form transference reactions to the group leader and to each other on the basis of their early life experiences. Thus, the interactions that occur in the group reflect personality structures and the use of defense mechanisms that members develop early in life. The group leader uses transference and counter transference reactions to help members work through unresolved conflicts by exploring past behavior patterns and linking these patterns to current behaviors. For instance, this theory explains as "sibling rivalry" the way two group members vy for the attention of the group leader. The development of insight into early life experiences and their effects is a key ingredient in Psychodynamic theory (Payne, 1997).

While the theories reviewed above are not an exhaustive list of those used by social work professionals, they are considered some of the common theories used in the practice of social work. For the purpose of developing and refining your group facilitation skills in this class, these should serve to support and inform your activities. In addition, you might find it necessary for particular exercises to review additional theories or alternative theories to prepare for your turn as a (co)facilitator.

SKILLS

Please use this simple table to review the essential skills for working with individuals and groups. These skills should be familiar to you from previous classes. It is important that you utilize and begin to internalize these skills as you facilitate your group exercise. They should become part of your natural behavior as a professional social worker. Just as you have a professional vocabulary, so too should you have a professional skill set. Again, this chart does not present a completely comprehensive list of all skills needed to (co)facilitate groups. It is however, a list of the key foundational skills that all beginning professionals should be able to exhibit at any given time. Please note that some authors/educators may use different names to represent the same skills.

GROUP AND INDIVIDUAL SKILLS

SKILL	DEFINITION
Seek to discover client strengths	It is important to identify client strengths in terms of competencies, successes, life's lessons, and social and cultural supports. When clients successfully use their own strengths to help with the resolution of their difficulties, it increases the likelihood that they may feel empowered and be more successful in future endeavors involving problem solving.
Closed ended questions	Closed ended questions are utilized to elicit short responses, often times yes/no responses. They can yield a great deal of information in a short period of time. They may be very useful during "crisis" work. Their use is dependent on the purpose of the meeting or the phase of the meeting. Too many questions of this sort may make the client feel like she/he is being interrogated. Closed ended questions may help people with limited expressive abilities to feel more comfortable early in an interview.
Open-ended questions	Open- ended questions are utilized to encourage people to express themselves expansively. These types of questions are most effective with people who have the ability to express themselves in a comprehensive manner and have the desire to do so. ***Be careful, in that questions can imply blame, judgment, and evaluation. Either–Or questions may be confusing to the client. Avoid leading questions, whether closed or open ended, as they do not serve a healthy purpose.
Seeking Clarification	Seeking clarification involves asking the client to elaborate and/or to be more specific about a recent statement. This may be necessary because you have not listened well, or the client has been vague or appeared to skip important parts of her/his story (or both). Seeking clarification is especially important if cultural factors are present. For example, Mr. Frank N. Stein says, "my three year old son throws 'temper tantrums' every afternoon". It is important that I, as the social worker, ask Mr. Stein something like this –"Could you tell me what a typical temper tantrum looks and sounds like?" By answering this question, Mr. Stein moves beyond the use of a label and actually describes what he sees and hears.
Simple Encouragement/ Parroting	This skill involves using well-timed non-verbal responses like a head nod or raising one's eyebrows as well as identifying a key word from the client's description of events and repeating it.
Reflecting Content	This is the empathetic skill of communicating your understanding of the factual or informational part of a client's message. It's a form of active listening achieved by briefly paraphrasing the client's factual or informational words. By accurately reflecting content you demonstrate that you have heard and understood what the client is attempting to convey. This is presumed to be most effective when the client has communicated factual material or ideas that may or may not include emotional content. This is much more effective than the dreaded use of the phrase "I understand" (*ugh.*).

Reflecting Feelings	This skill is a parallel of reflecting content. As with reflecting content, reflecting feelings is another example of empathic active listening skills. It often consists of a brief response that includes key feeling words of the client and communicates your understanding of the feelings or emotions expressed by a client. Some of the most effective ways to communicate reflection of feeling is with simple statements"YOU FEEL _____". To do this effectively, it is important to have a readily available vocabulary of terms that connote emotions at different levels of intensity. Different cultural groups and individuals will have different sets of feeling words or manner of implying feelings.
Reflecting Content and Feeling	This skill combines both of the previous skills and involves the use of key client words that reflect emotional and informational elements of a message. Do not speculate or interpret about the client's meaning or intentions, but rather use key elements of a client's statement.
Paraphrasing or Rephrasing (*similar to Reflecting Content*)	This skill involves verbalizing the essence of what the client has said by abbreviating and clarifying client comments. It involves using some of your own words and the key words of the client. Good use of paraphrasing moves the client on to new issues or deeper meaning by validating what she/he has said.
Summarizing	The skill of summarizing covers a longer time span, perhaps an entire meeting, and includes more information than paraphrasing and reflecting content and feeling. This skill may be used to set the context for beginning an interview or ending one. It may serve as a transition to a new topic or to clarify lengthy and complex client issues. Summarizations help clients organize their thinking. A "Checkout" at the end of the summarizing, paraphrasing, and reflecting content and feeling is important.
Partializing	The skill of partializing involves breaking down distinct aspects and dimensions of a client's communication into more manageable parts in order to address them more easily. This skill helps your client and you maintain a sense of coherence by exploring smaller, more manageable units of information one at a time. The skill of partializing may be used as a pre-requisite to prioritizing the importance of several issues.
Going beyond	This skill involves your use of your empathic understanding of the other person to extend slightly what she or he had actually said. Instead of repeating what the client has said, you use your knowledge, experience and practice wisdom to add modestly to the feelings or meanings actually communicated. Through a process sometimes called additive empathy, you take a small leap beyond the spoken word to bring into greater awareness or clarity information the client already knows. In other words, your responses go beyond what the client has explicitly stated to what was implied or perhaps indicated through non-verbal communication. Going beyond involves putting into words those thoughts and feelings that a person probably already feels or thinks but has not yet expressed. For instance, a client tightly gripping the arm of a chair while telling their story may indicate the presence of anxiety of some sort that they have not expressed or may not be fully aware. Like other skills in this list, the skill of going beyond should be expressed tentatively and followed with a "check out".

Checkouts	A question, asked of a client, following the use of such skills as seeking clarification, partializing, reflecting content and/or feelings, paraphrasing, summarizing, and going beyond. For example "Is that correct?" etc.
Universalizing	This is the skill of helping members become aware of the similarities of their personal issues to those of other group members. This often involves restating issues of several clients at a higher level of abstraction. For instance, group members may have discussed the following issues: "I'm lonely," "I have trouble making friends," "my partner and I just don't talk to one another anymore," and "I feel all alone in the world". The social worker may universalize these statements by identifying a possible theme regarding how important it is for us as human beings to connect with one another. The skill of universalizing helps individual clients see how their own issue is connected to others in the group. The skill of universalizing serves the broader goal of developing group cohesion.
Agenda Setting	Having an explicit agenda is important, regardless of whether you are facilitating task or intervention/treatment groups. Even for psychodynamically oriented treatment groups, members need to know its purpose, and start times and end times. For most groups, an explicit agenda will facilitate individual and group goal achievement. Written agendas are the best way to provide structure for group meetings. However, the key issue is that the agenda is explicit. So, if a group facilitator chooses not to use a written agenda, then it is incumbent upon her/him to verbally set a clear agenda for group members. Agendas may include the answers to the questions: "What has the group and its members accomplished during the last meeting?" the "Who will do what, when?" for the current meeting and "What to expect during the next meeting?" Agendas for task groups should include all specific activities of the meeting while agendas for intervention/treatment groups may be somewhat less structured and include only a time allotment for all planned activities. Using a timeframe for completion of certain types of treatment group activities provides structure but allows individuals within the group some choices about how they may participate in within a given timeframe.
Group Decision Making	All groups use one decision-making model or another. However, it's not uncommon for group members to no be unaware of the model until a decision is made, which they may not like. It is a matter of good ethical practice for social workers facilitating groups to ensure that the decision-making model that is going to be used is transparent to all group members. Moreover, group members should be involved in determining a decision making model to the greatest extent reasonably possible.
Concluding Comments Regarding Group Skills	The characteristics of group members and the distribution of those characteristics will influence the use of all of the previously mentioned skills, as well as non-verbal skills such as eye contact, head nodding, posturing, use of hands, proximity, mirroring, and/or complimentary positioning. As a group leader, we have several primary tasks. One is to foster maximum individual participation, while another is to foster equal opportunity for all to participate. Power relationships outside of the group will no doubt influence group member interactions within the group. Those group members who have membership in one or more disenfranchised groups and those group members who have primary membership in one of more dominant groups may replicate these power dynamics in the group if the leader unwittingly lets this happen.

STAGES OF GROUP DEVELOPMENT
(Adapted from Toseland & Rivas, 2009; Corey, 2008)

Just to be sure you have this information at your disposal, we've developed the following table to help you review the key stages of group development. As you have learned already, these stages may look different, occur differently, and last differing lengths of time depending upon the type of group, the environment in which you are doing your work, and the composition of your members. It will be important that you understand the implications of group functioning at any one of these stages, as some of the exercises in this text instruct the (co)facilitators to start in a particular stage of the group and that stage certainly has implications for how the group members and leaders will behave.

Key Issues in group development	A group's entire social structure, its communication and interaction patterns, cohesion, social controls, and culture evolve over time. There is general agreement that groups move through progressive stages, including, in general, beginning, middle, and end stages. It's also widely held that groups move backwards from time to time to redress certain basic issues or processes. Movement through theses stages of group development is most readily seen in closed membership groups that are time limited. Open membership groups that do not have an end date likely do not move progressively through all of these stages. Those that change membership most often tend to make less progress through these stages. It is noteworthy, that while an open ended and open membership group may not move through all of the previously mentioned stages of group development, individual members may still experience meaningful progression through these stages on an individual basis.
Characteristics of Beginning Stage	This is a time for orientation, forming, and planning. Members are concerned about trust and safety issues. There may be ambivalence, resistance, power and control issues. At the beginning of this stage, members are often unsure of their roles, group rules and group norms. As members move through this stage and norms and roles begin to become apparent, members test these out. It is not uncommon for there to be conflict during these times. This is a natural process for the group and with a competent group leader, serves as preparation for healthy working relationships in the middle phase of the group.
Characteristics of Middle Stage	This is a time for the development of more mature and productive working relationships. It may include negotiation, conflict, and evaluating, along with the development of greater intimacy, trust, cohesion, and goal achievement. As a group progressively moves to the middle phase, the group (including a competent group facilitator), develops more stable ways of interacting, greater interpersonal attraction and group cohesion, and shows a strong movement toward group and individual goals.
Characteristics of Ending Stage	This is a time for decision-making, separation, and **termination** concurrent with a decline in a sense of cohesion. This stage includes the completion of group and individual goals to the greatest extent possible, or finishing of their business. This is also a time to summarize the group's accomplishments, evaluate both the work of the group and its individual members, and perhaps to celebrate the group's work.

Brief Checklist of Items to Remember When Facilitating a Group

As a final reminder, we've developed this brief checklist for you as you prepare to (co)facilitate an exercise with your peers. Remember, you've been exposed to essential content, you've done your own research, you've consulted your instructor and the resources provided in this text…and you're ready to go!

1. Know the purpose of the group

2. Know the stage of the group

3. Have an agenda

4. Be aware of the relationship between the theories and skills of group work

5. Don't forget the NASW Code of Ethics

6. Know the limits of your competence

7. Be aware of the influence of culture and power upon group member relationships

8. Make sure the physical environment fosters a healthy group atmosphere

9. Take slow deep breaths to help calm yourself

10. Start your group on time

11. Use your social work skills to foster a healthy group environment and individual participation

12. Don't be afraid of brief periods of silence--it may give clients time to talk about what they are thinking and feeling

13. Encourage group member autonomy to the greatest extent possible given the type of group, stage of group, and group composition

14. End your group on time

SECTION 2

OPEN MEMBERSHIP TREATMENT GROUPS

CHAPTER 2

A GROUP PRACTICE EXERCISE WITH

LESBIAN, GAY, BI-SEXUAL, TRANSGENDER, INTERSEX, AND QUEER/QUESTIONING (LGBTIQ) ADOLESCENTS "COMING OUT"

STEPHEN ERICH & HEATHER KANENBERG

By the end of this exercise, you should be able to demonstrate:

- Evidence of theoretical knowledge of group functioning through your performance in the in-class group facilitation exercise.

- Evidence of theoretical knowledge of the LGBTIQ community through your performance in the in-class group facilitation exercise.

- Knowledge of terminology appropriate for working with this community.

- Evidence of competence related to the use of group work skills via the in-class group facilitation exercise.

BEFORE YOU BEGIN

The purpose of this exercise is to introduce students to group practice issues and experiences when working with members of the LGBTIQ community. It will be important that you take time both in and out of class to prepare for such a task.

A bit of background to aid in your preparation: This group exercise assumes students will have been exposed to essential theoretical content, including theory specifically related to the LGBTIQ community, LGBTIQ identity development, and issues related to the coming-out process. You are also expected to be familiar with language appropriate for working with this community, as well as theory and skills relevant to the facilitation of therapeutic groups. This chapter, as described here, is a one or two-class period process, depending on whether theoretical content is presented in the current class or a previous one. Your instructor may modify this exercise to best meet your needs.

If you don't consider yourself familiar with this information or prepared for the exercise, you'll need to review some of this essential content in order to improve your effectiveness. Feel free to use the web resources at the end of the exercise, the initial chapters of the book, the bibliography at the end of the text, your other textbooks, and your instructor as resources to help you prepare.

GROUP EXERCISE:
LESBIAN, GAY, BISEXUAL, TRANSGENDER, INTERSEX AND QUEER/QUESTIONING (LGBTIQ) ADOLESCENTS "COMING OUT"

You and one of your peers will facilitate a support/education group for a portion of the class period (typically 45-60 minutes).

SCENARIO

You and your co-leader (optional) are BSWs leading a support/educational group for lesbian, gay, bisexual, transgender, intersex, and queer/questioning adolescents. The purpose of this group is to support the development of a positive identity and self-esteem among members. Parents have signed a fairly non-descript consent form allowing their children to participate in the group. Common issues include family relationships, peer relationships, affectional/sexual relationships, the coming-out process, loneliness and isolation, spiritual/religious issues, community attitudes, other sources of support, etc. This group is sponsored by Parents and Friends of Lesbians and Gays (PFLAG).

The group meets weekly for 45-60 minutes and has already met on several occasions. This is an open group, thus new members may enter the group at different times. The group is also open-ended (not limited to a specific number of sessions). The group consists of veteran members (those who have attended several sessions) as well as a couple of newcomers (both having attended only one session). All group members are between the ages of 15 and 18. The group has expressed an interest in talking about coming-out issues. How to do it? Who to come out to? When to come out? Should they come out? What worked and what did not seem to work so well? **You and your co-leader have the task of facilitating this discussion.**

GROUP FACILITATOR TASKS

You and your co-leader are BSWs leading a support/educational group for lesbian, gay, bi-sexual, transgender, intersex, and queer/questioning adolescents.

1) To begin, you and your co-facilitator will want to conduct some research to develop your identity and some context for this role. *See the Character Profile assignment in Group Member Section.*

2) Prior to the group, you will need to develop an agenda for your group meeting. Feel free to use the following space to develop your agenda with your co-leader.   If you need some assistance, review the "Before you Begin" and "Scenario" portions of the exercise. You can also use the sample agendas in Appendix 1 as a guide. You will need to make the agenda available to your members in some way. You can post the agenda or distribute a copy of it to each participant on the day of the exercise (feel free to be creative with how this is done). You can also talk with your instructor about this.

_____

_____

_____

_____

_____

_____

_____

_____

_____

_____

_____

_____

_____

_____

_____

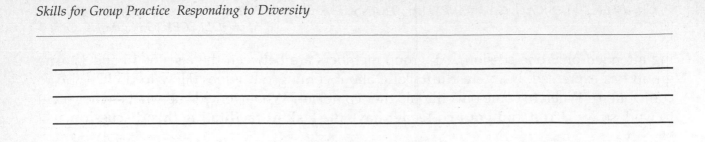

You will want to keep in mind all or many of the following points while the group is in session:

- Create an environment conducive to healthy communication and understanding.
- Introduce group members, if necessary.
- Cover/review confidentiality and group rules, procedures, and roles, if necessary.
- Prepare, explain, and discuss the structure of today's meeting: "Issues Related to Coming Out."
- Use skills to foster understanding of the purpose and goals of the group.
- Use skills to facilitate task accomplishment within the group.
- Respond purposely to questions, comments, and concerns of members.
- Facilitate the group process-using the available skill set.
- Develop and implement your plan for ending this group session.

ROLES FOR GROUP MEMBERS

Prior to the beginning of the group, you with the assistance of your instructor, will get yourself "centered," if necessary, so that you will be able to engage in role playing as members of the Coming Out Group.

1) In this exercise, there are several participants, but no identified roles or character descriptions for them. **Before you start**, get together with the other members to identify your role and character. Keep in mind there are some expectations that some members will be younger adolescents concerned with '"coming out" and some will be older adolescents in the "coming out" group. You will want to assume the identity and story of the member you choose prior to the group exercise. To help you become more acquainted with your role, develop a **character profile** about the person you are playing, describing the character, her/his age and "story," how she/he came to join the group, and her/his status in the group.

As you develop your character, we encourage you to ensure diversity is present in all its many forms within the group. As you consider who you will be and what your concerns are, consider whether or not you will represent an oppressed group. Are you an adolescent with physical limitations, hearing loss, or from a single parent family? Perhaps you will play the role of an adolescent that is emancipated, or a client in the juvenile justice system, or maybe English is not your native language? **Please consult your instructor as you develop your character prior to the group exercise.**

Character: _____

_____

_____

_____

_____

_____

_____

_____

_____

_____

_____

You will also want to function in a genuine manner while the group is in session. For instance, if you are unclear about something said by the facilitator(s),   you should express yourself honestly and seek clarity.

OBSERVER TASKS

Your role for this exercise is that of an **observer**. You have had or will have a chance to facilitate or participate in an exercise in your class, but during this group process experience you should sit quietly around the perimeter of the group. You will be assessing the performance of the group facilitators and at a later time you will share your professional observations with other group exercise participants.

1) Use the following chart to help with your expectations and observations. Here are some questions to get you started:"What do you expect will take place during this group?""What do you expect to see the facilitators doing?""Which social work knowledge, values, and skills do you expect to be present in this 'coming out' group meeting?" "Are there concepts of group practice that you think will be particularly helpful to the facilitators as they conduct their work?"

Expectations Before the Group Session	Observations During the Group Session
Knowledge:	Knowledge:
Skills:	Skills:
Values:	Values:
Other:	Other:

REFLECTING ON THE GROUP SESSION

A critical portion of this learning exercise is the processing that takes place immediately after the exercise. At the end of the group, all students will have the opportunity to participate in a post-group reflection exercise. The purpose of this reflection is to process the experiences of the group session and to make meaning of what transpired.

This process typically begins with the student group facilitators describing their experience leading the group. **Group facilitators**, you are expected to share the thoughts and emotions that you experienced during the group. Most importantly, you will provide a critique of your work that includes a **balanced assessment** of your strengths and areas for improvement. Then, each **participating group member**, including the joker(s), should use the "round robin" technique to provide balanced feedback for the facilitators. Lastly, the **observers** will comment on the exercise.

All members of the class (facilitators, group members, observers, and jokers) should consider the knowledge, skills, and values that were demonstrated during the group exercise. In addition, feedback and reflection upon what was absent during the experience that perhaps could have fostered group progress will make for meaningful group discussion.   Our hope for you during this reflection exercise is that you are able to consider your own skills and the skills of your colleagues in context with what you've learned thus far in your curriculum and in this course in particular.

SUMMARY, KEY CONCEPTS, AND PRINCIPLES

You have just had the unique experience of participating in a support/educational group for lesbian, gay, bi-sexual, transgender, intersex, and queer/questioning adolescents.   Hopefully this exercise was interesting and contributed to your understanding of the complexities of group work. As you take time to reflect on the session and the social work knowledge, skills, and values that were manifested in the experience, you might consider any one or more of the following key concepts and principles:

Trust and Safety
LGBTIQ identity development
Group norms and roles
Power within the group
Multicultural perspectives

Feminist Theory
Queer theory
Identity development
Group Cohesion
NASW Code of Ethics

WEB RESOURCES

Human Rights Campaign
http://www.hrc.org/. The Human Rights Campaign. The HRC also has a section of its webpage devoted to issues impacting the Lesbian, Gay, Bisexual, Transgender/Transsexual community:http://www. hrc. org/Template.cfm? Section=Transgender_Issues1
- There is information available regarding:
- The Local Law Enforcement Act
- A state law database to determine which states have protections for people based on sexual orientation and gender identity
- A checklist for becoming a better advocate for Transgender Inclusion
- Tools for managers to ensure LGBTI equality in the workplace

Parents, Family, and Friends of Lesbian and Gays (PFLAG)
http://www.pflag.org/. Parents, Family and Friends of Lesbians and Gays (PFLAG).

The Transgender Law and Policy Institute
http://www.transgenderlaw.org/. The Transgender Law and Policy Institute.
- Federal legislation
- State legislation
- Advocacy efforts

- Case law
- University policies
- Employer and union policies

Ohio State University Transgender Guide
http://multiculturalcenter.osu.edu/glbtss. Ohio State University Transgender Guide & Resource Center. Ohio State University, through its Multicultural Center, has an extensive resource page for students that provides education and promotes inclusion and equity.

Gender Center Inc.
http://www.gendercentre.org.au/index1.htm. Gender Centre Inc. – Sydney Australia. The Gender Centre is committed to developing and providing services and activities that enhance the ability of people working with, serving or experiencing issues related to gender to make informed choices. There is also a portion of the website dedicated to human resource policy and Transgender individuals.
http://www.gendercentre.org.au/human_resource_po licy.htm

Intersex Society of North America (ISNA)
http://www.insa.org. Intersex Society of North America (ISNA).

CHAPTER 3

A GROUP PRACTICE EXERCISE WITH

SCHOOL-BASED SOCIAL WORK WITH AT-RISK ADOLESCENTS

STEPHEN ERICH & HEATHER KANENBERG

By the end of this exercise, you should be able to demonstrate:

- Theoretical knowledge of group functioning as evidenced by your performance in the in-class group facilitation exercise.

- Evidence of theoretical knowledge of adolescent development, particularly younger adolescents (12-15).

- Awareness and understanding of the National Association of Social Workers Code of Ethics through your performance in the in-class group facilitation exercise. In particular, the limits of confidentiality, assent/consent, and risk assessment.

- Knowledge of terminology appropriate for working with this community.

- Evidence of competence related to the use of group work skills via the in-class group facilitation exercise.

BEFORE YOU BEGIN

The purpose of this exercise is to introduce students to group practice issues and experiences when working with adolescents in a school- based setting. It will be important that you take time both in and out of class to prepare for such a task. It is expected that you will have been exposed to theory and information related to school-based social worker's roles.

As a bit of background to aid in your preparation: As is common practice, the facilitator(s) of this scenario are not employees of the school district, but actually employed by a non-profit agency that serves at-risk teens. The physical plant of the school houses the employees of the agency. Moreover, employees must be aware of not only their own agency's policies and procedures, but the school district's as well. This group experience assumes students will have been exposed to essential theoretical content including adolescent development and risk assessment as well as ethical issues, especially those associated with consent/assent, limits of confidentiality, and competence. Students are also expected to be familiar with language appropriate for working with this community, as well as theory and skills relevant to the facilitation of therapeutic groups. The exercise, as described here, is a one or two-class period process, depending on whether theoretical content is presented in the current class or a previous one. Instructors should feel free to modify this exercise in ways that best meets the needs of their students.

If you don't consider yourself familiar with this information or prepared for the exercise, you'll need to review some of this essential content in order to advance in your effectiveness. Feel free to use the web resources at the end of the exercise, the initial chapters of the book, the bibliography at the end of the text, your other textbooks, and also your instructor as resources to help you prepare.

GROUP EXERCISE:
SCHOOL-BASED SOCIAL WORK WITH AT-RISK ADOLESCENTS

You and one of your peers will facilitate a support/education group for a portion of the class period (typically 45-60 minutes).

SCENARIO

You and your co-leader (optional) are BSWs leading a support/educational group for at-risk adolescents (12-15). **The purpose of this group** is to support the development of a positive identity and self-esteem among members. Common issues include family relationships, peer relationships, affectional/sexual relationships, loneliness and isolation, spiritual/religious issues, community attitudes, etc.

It is understood by all students that the group has met on several occasions. It meets weekly for one hour. **This is an open group**, thus new members may enter the group at different times. The group is also open-ended (not limited to a specific number of sessions). **The group**

consists of teens who have been in the group for different lengths of time. The group is scheduled to discuss relationships with parents. You and your co-leader have the task of facilitating this discussion.

GROUP FACILITATOR TASKS

You and your co-leader are BSWs leading a support/educational group for at risk adolescents in a school setting.

1) To begin, you and your co-facilitator will want to conduct some research to develop your identity and some context for this role. *See Character Profile assignment in Group Member Section.*

2) Prior to the group, you will need to develop an agenda for your group meeting. Jot down some ideas of what you will need to include in your agenda. Feel free to use the following space to develop your agenda with your co-leader. If you need some assistance, review the "Before you Begin" and "Scenario" portions of the exercise. You can also use the sample agendas in Appendix 1 as a guide. You will need to make the agenda available to your members in some way. You can post the agenda or distribute a copy of it to each participant on the day of the exercise (feel free to be creative with how this is done). Talk with your instructor if you have questions.

_____

_____

_____

_____

_____

_____

_____

_____

_____

_____

_____

_____

_____

You will want to keep in mind all or most of the following points while the group is in session:

- Create an environment conducive to healthy communication and understanding.
- Introduce group members, if necessary.
- If necessary, discuss/review confidentiality and group rules, procedures, risk assessment and roles.
- Prepare, explain, and discuss the structure of today's meeting.
- Use skills to foster understanding of the purpose and goals of the group.
- Use skills to facilitate task accomplishment within the group.
- Respond purposely to questions, comments, and concerns of members.
- Facilitate the group process by using the available skill set.
- Develop and implement your plan for ending this group session.

ROLES FOR GROUP MEMBERS

Prior to the beginning of the group, you, with the assistance of your instructor, will get yourself "centered" if necessary, so that you will be able to engage in role playing as members of the support/education group for at-risk adolescents.

1) In this exercise, there are several participants, but no identified roles or character descriptions for them. **Before you start**, get together with the other members to identify your role and character. Keep in mind group members should identify as younger adolescents. You will want to be sure this is understood by all participants as you and your classmates select your role and develop your identity. You will want to assume the identity and story of the member you choose prior to the group exercise. To help you become more acquainted with your role, develop a **character profile** about the person you are playing, describing the character, her/his age and "story," and her/his status in the group.

As you develop your character, we encourage you to ensure diversity is present in all its many forms within the group. As you consider who you will be and your concerns, consider whether or not you will represent an oppressed group. Are you an adolescent with limited intellectual functioning (IQ 70-80), or are you from a single parent family? Perhaps you will play the role of an adolescent that is emancipated, or a client in the juvenile justice system, or maybe English is not your first language. **Please consult your instructor as you develop your character prior to the group exercise.**

Character: _____

_____

_____

_____

_____

_____

_____

_____

_____

_____

_____

You will also want to behave in a genuine manner while the group is in session. For instance, if you are unclear about something the facilitator(s) say, then you should express yourself honestly and seek clarity.

OBSERVER TASKS

Your role for this exercise is that of an **observer**. You have had or will have a chance to facilitate or participate in an exercise in your class, but during this group process experience you should sit quietly around the perimeter of the group. You will be assessing the performance of the group facilitators and at a later time will share your professional observations with other group exercise participants.

1) Use the following chart to help with your expectations and observations. Here are some questions to get you started: What do you expect to take place during this group session? What do you expect to see the facilitators doing? Which social work knowledge, values, and skills do you expect to be present in this at-risk adolescent support/educational group meeting? Are there concepts of group practice that you think will be particularly helpful to the facilitators as they conduct their work?

Expectations Before the Group Session	Observations During the Group Session
Knowledge:	Knowledge:
Skills:	Skills:
Values:	Values:
Other:	Other:

REFLECTING ON THE GROUP SESSION

A critical portion of this learning exercise is the processing that takes place immediately after the exercise. At the end of the group, all students will have the opportunity to participate in a post-group reflection exercise. The purpose of this reflection is to process the experiences of the group session and to understand the meaning of what transpired.

This process typically begins with the student group facilitators describing their experience leading the group. **Group facilitators**: you are expected to share the thoughts and emotions that you experienced during the group. Most importantly, you will provide a critique of your work that includes a **balanced assessment** of your strengths and areas for improvement. Then, each **participating group member**, including the joker(s), should use the 'round robin' technique to provide balanced feedback for the facilitators. Lastly, the **observers** will comment on the exercise.

All members of the class (facilitators, group members, observers, and jokers) should consider the knowledge, skills and values that were demonstrated during the group exercise. In addition, feedback and reflection upon what was absent during the experience that perhaps could have assisted with group progress will make for meaningful group discussion. We hope that during this reflection exercise you are able to consider your own skills and the skills of your colleagues in context with what you've learned thus far in your curriculum and in this course in particular.

SUMMARY, KEY CONCEPTS, AND PRINCIPLES

You have just had the unique experience of participating in a support/educational group for at-risk adolescents in a school setting. Hopefully this exercise was interesting and contributed to your understanding of the complexities of group work. As you take time to reflect on the session and the social work knowledge, skills, and values that were manifested in the experience, you might consider any one or all of the following key concepts and principles:

Group norms and roles   Conflict Theory
Ecological Theory   Identity Development (younger adolescents)
Systems Theory   Group Cohesion
Multicultural perspectives   NASW Code of Ethics
Empowerment   • Consent/assent
Strengths perspectives   • Limits of confidentiality
Feminist Theory   • Compliance
Queer Theory   • Risk Assessment

WEB RESOURCES

After-School All-Stars
http://www.afterschoolallstars.org/site/pp.asp?c=enJJ
KMNpFmG&b=854685
After School All Stars offers a proven alternative for middle school children. We engage them in activities and on-going relationships that increase confidence and encourage success in all areas of their lives — at home, in school and in the community.

All our Kids, Inc.
http://www.allourkids.org/
Mentors of All Our Kids come from all walks of life; however, their commonality is helping at-risk kids. From college students to retirees, all mentors share the desire to help a child succeed. Each potential mentor is screened with an interview, driving record and a criminal background check.

Center for Assessment and Policy Development
http://www.capd.org/pubfiles/pub-1996-10-06.pdf
School-based programs for adolescent parents and their young children. A PDF document produced by the CAPD for guidelines for quality and best practice.

Communities in Schools
http://www.cisnet.org/about/who.asp
For 30 years, CIS has championed the connection of needed community resources with schools. By bringing caring adults into the schools to address children's unmet needs, CIS provides the link between educators and the community. The result: Teachers are free to teach, and students — many in jeopardy of dropping out — finally have the opportunity to focus on learning.

National Association of Social Workers (NASW)
http://www.naswdc.org/pubs/code/default.asp
The NASW Code of Ethics is intended to serve as a guide to the everyday professional conduct of social workers. This Code includes four sections. The first Section, "Preamble," summarizes the social work profession's mission and core values. The second section, "Purpose of the NASW Code of Ethics," provides an overview of the Code's main functions and a brief guide for dealing with ethical issues or dilemmas in social work practice. The third section, "Ethical Principles," presents broad ethical principles, based on social work's core values that inform social work

practice. The final section, "Ethical Standards," includes specific ethical standards to guide social workers' conduct and to provide a basis for adjudication.

National Institute on Drug Abuse (NIDA)
http://www.nida.nih.gov/NIDA_notes/NNVol12N3/Specialized.html

Adolescents on their way to dropping out of school and abusing drugs can be diverted toward healthier, more successful lives, according to NIDA-supported researchers. By using interventions designed specifically to address the personal and social factors that place some high school students at risk of drug abuse, schools can reduce these young people's drug use and other unhealthy behaviors, these researchers say.

CHAPTER 4

A GROUP PRACTICE EXERCISE WITH

AFRICAN AMERICANS LIVING WITH HIV/AIDS

YVONNE OKONKWO, STEPHEN ERICH
& HEATHER KANENBERG

By the end of this exercise, you should be able to demonstrate:

- Theoretical knowledge of group functioning through your performance in the in-class group facilitation exercise.

- Theoretical knowledge of the African American community through your performance in the in-class group facilitation exercise.

- Knowledge of terminology appropriate for working with HIV positive African Americans living openly in their given communities.

- Evidence of competence related to the use of group skills via the in class facilitation exercise.

- Knowledge of NASW's Code of Ethics and Association for Advancement of Social Work with Groups Standard's for Social Work practice and will implement these guidelines in practice.

- Appropriate action when dealing with isolates, scapegoats, as well as legal issues, including confidentiality and confronting intense subgroups.

BEFORE YOU BEGIN

The purpose of this module is to introduce you to group practice issues and real life experiences when working with members of the African American Community living openly with HIV/AIDS. This chapter assumes that you will have been exposed to essential theoretical content related to working with non-dominate groups, persons of color, the culturally diverse, HIV issues, confidentiality and legal HIV/AIDS related issues. This exercise is a one or two class period process, depending on whether or not theoretical content is presented in the previous class settings. Your instructor will modify the exercise to best meet the needs of your learning goals. It will be important that you take time both in and out of class to prepare for this task. As a bit of background to aid in your preparation:

According to the 2000 census, Blacks made up approximately thirteen percent of the U.S. population; however, in 2005 Blacks (including African Americans) accounted for 20,187 (50%) of the estimated 40,608 AIDS cases diagnosed in the 50 states and the District of Columbia (Centers for Disease Control [CDC], 2007). Moreover, Blacks accounted for nearly half (49%) of the estimated new HIV/AIDS diagnoses in 33 states with long term confidential name-based HIV reporting (CDC, 2007). Furthermore, according to the Southern AIDS Coalition (2008) of the 20 metropolitan areas with the highest rates of AIDS cases in 2006, 16 were in the South. Additionally, the statistics are more troubling in the east coast. The AIDS rate in Washington, D.C. is an alarming nine times the national average (O'Brien, 2008). According to the Black AIDS Institute (2008), in Washington D.C., Black Americans account for eighty percent of HIV cases. That is one in 20 residents or 5% of the entire population is infected with this disease (O'Brien, 2008; Fauci, 2008). Dr. Anthony Fauci (2008) of the National Institute of Allergy and Infectious Diseases told CNN for the 2008 "Black in America" documentary that the rate of African Americans infected with HIV is "comparable to countries like Uganda or South Africa". Therefore, Phil Wilson (2008), founder of the Black AIDS Institute, has stated, "AIDS in America today is a Black disease". Given these alarming statistics, it is inevitable that all mental health practitioners will come in contact with a client who is HIV positive, or is closely related to someone who has acquired HIV/AIDS. This exercise will focus on working with African Americans living openly with HIV/AIDS—in particular African American females newly infected with HIV (among the 49% of Blacks living with HIV/AIDS, 64% were Black women).

The reasons for the disproportionate HIV/AIDS rate in the African American community have stemmed from collective denial and ambivalence, combined with misconception that the disease is completely curable, stigma and myths around those who contract the disease (O'Brien, 2008). Moreover, according to the Centers for Disease Control and Prevention (2007), Black women are most likely to be infected with HIV/AIDS as a result of sex with male partners' with possible risk factors for HIV infection, such as unprotected sex with multiple partners, bisexuality, or injection drug use (Journal of the American Medicaid Association, 2001; Journal of the National Medical Association, 2005). In addition, male-to-male sexual contact was the primary risk factor for 48% of Black men with HIV/AIDS at the end of 2005, and high-risk heterosexual contact was the primary risk factor for 22% (CDC, 2007). Moreover, socioeconomic issues and other social and structural influences affect the rates of HIV infection among Blacks (National Minority AIDS Council, 2006). The biopsychosocial structural influences include minimal access to comprehensive and preventive healthcare, lack of education and poverty.

This therapeutic group can be a critical support system during the troubled experiences your clients will likely endure which includes: episodes of anxiety, anger, and fear of rejection; judgment from their loved ones, family members, community and society as a whole.

If you don't consider yourself familiar with this information or prepared for the exercise, you'll need to review some of this essential content in order to aid in your effectiveness. Feel free to use the web resources at the end of the exercise, the initial chapters of the book, the bibliography at the end of the text, your other textbooks, and also your instructor as resources to help you prepare.

GROUP EXERCISE:
AFRICAN AMERICANS LIVING WITH HIV/AIDS

You and your co-leader are BSW's leading a support/growth/social skills group for African Americans diagnosed with HIV/AIDS in a privately funded, non-profit community agency (typically 45 minutes – 1 hour).

As the group leader, your goal is to meet the socio-emotional needs of the group members (Toseland & Rivas, 2009). When working with African Americans living with HIV/AIDS openly in the community, it is important to be mindful of the pervasive stigma attached to the disease. Moreover, as a group leader, when working with non-voluntary clients it is critical to meet the client where they are. This could be addressed by incorporating the reciprocal model, in which the group leader acts in part as the mediator, helping group members find the common ground between their bio/psycho/social/spiritual needs as African Americans living with HIV/AIDS in the open community and their respective demands from their families and community (Toseland & Rivas, 2009).

Granted, this exercise explores the group dynamics when working with African Americans who are living with HIV/AIDS in the open community; however, you must acknowledge (or be cognizant) that every group member will not be completely open about their health status to potential third party victims, cooperative in the group process, or assertive in group participation. A person living with HIV/AIDS is not obligated by law to reveal her/his health status to the public. However, as a mental health professional, you have a responsibility to protect the public from potentially dangerous clients and to protect your client from themselves (Corey, Corey, & Callanan, 2007).

Moreover, as social workers we have an ethical obligation to protect our client's confidentiality (National Association of Social Workers, 1999). Nevertheless, there are legal and ethical considerations to HIV/AIDS-related cases and issues. Corey, Corey, and Callanan (2007) maintain that the guidelines to when confidentiality may be breached remains unclear. They have stated that "Courts have yet applied the duty to warn to cases involving HIV infection, and therapists' legal responsibility in protecting sexual partners of HIV-positive clients" (2007, p. 251). Given this fact social workers are likely not allowed to inform potential third party victims but may feel justified to breach confidentiality, you, and your co-leader must be clear with all group members from the outset about all limits to confidentiality, including dealing with HIV-positive clients who are unwilling to inform their sexual partners of their HIV status. In addition, Corey, Corey, and Callanan (2007) advise social workers to consult with a supervisor or an attorney because they "may be subject to liability for either failure to warn those entitled to warnings or warning those who are not entitled" (p.225). It is imperative to know your legal opportunities and obligations given that they vary state by state. For instance, practicing Licensed Clinical Social Worker Chino Okonkwo points out that in the state of New York counselors fill out a form to notify potential their party victims to the state, and then the state of New York notifies these potential victims.

Secondly, as group leaders, you may encounter group members who feel pressure or coerced to enter the therapeutic group therapy (Toseland & Rivas, 2009). Involuntary members who have joined the group by mandate may be resistant and exhibit ambivalent feelings to the process. Toseland and Rivas (2009) point out those ambivalent feelings toward change are common and generally a part of the therapeutic process; hence, they should not be looked at as an obstacle. Moreover, mandated clients may not be as open or participative as voluntary clients. Nevertheless, Yalom (2005) maintains that adequate preparation may likely ameliorate some of the negative feelings involuntary members have when they join the group. According to Toseland & Rivas (2005), the group leader has the opportunity to "help members work through their ambivalence and resistance and also help members work with each other to recognize where points of resistance may occur and to overcome challenges to their full participation" (p. 211).

Finally, as a group leader you'll want to be mindful of strong subgroups such as dyads, triads, and cliques that may form during the group process. As group facilitators, you'll want to be knowledgeable about strong subgroups that may deteriorate the integrity of the group as a whole and disrupt the cohesion of the group. You will also want to be aware of the presence of scapegoats and safeguard them from possible inappropriate criticism and blame from the group. In an ideal situation your student group members will facilitate the direction of the group that initiates and promotes the participation of isolates and new group members in order to gain the many advantages of the group process.

SCENARIO

The purpose of this group is to connect members to resources and services available in their community; provide support in a therapeutic environment; and also to ensure clients living with HIV/AIDS reach optimum adaptation, coping and social skills. Common issues include the following: family relationships, partner relationships, social exclusion, racial and gender inequality, risky sexual behavior, homophobia/transphobia, concealment of homosexual behavior, HIV/AIDS status disclosure, self-esteem, spirituality/religiosity, fear, grief, loss, depression, isolation, suicidal ideations, community support or alienation, socioeconomic status, class, and social justice. This group is sponsored by the Black Aids Institute and the National Minority AIDS Council.

It is understood by all students that the group has met on several occasions. The group meets weekly for 1 hour. **This is an open-ended group.** The group consist of veteran members who are living openly with HIV/AIDS for 5+ years, members who have been diagnosed within a year and have attended a couple of sessions, and one newcomer who is recently diagnosed and attends her first session during this particular group experience. Some group members come by choice or referral from other mental health professionals who are not competent with working with culturally diverse clients living with HIV/AIDS, and other members are former Injection Drug Users (IDU's) mandated to attend sessions by the state and their respective judges' rulings as a stipulation of their treatment /rehabilitation sentence. The heterogeneous makeup of the group consists of male and female HIV positive African Americans ranging from ages 18 to 40. Legality issues of self-disclosure, self-confidence, and assertiveness have been raised in today's session. Some individual group members are going through stages that include testing, conflict, and adjustment (Toseland & Rivas, 2009). **You and your co-leader have the task of addressing your clients' issues, questions, and concerns**.

GROUP FACILITATOR TASKS

You and your co-leader are BSW's leading a support/growth/social skills group for African Americans diagnosed with HIV/AIDS in a privately funded, non-profit community agency.

1) To begin, you and your co-facilitator will want to conduct some research to develop your identity and some context for this role. *See the Character Profile assignment in Group Member Section.*

2) Prior to the group, you will need to develop an agenda of some form for your members. Jot down some ideas of what you will need to include in your agenda. Feel free to use the following space to develop your agenda with your co-leader. If you need some assistance, review the "Before you Begin" and "Scenario" portions of the exercise. You can also use the sample agendas in Appendix 1 as a guide. You will need to make the agenda available to your members in some way. You can post the agenda, or distribute a copy of it to each participant on the day of the exercise (feel free to be creative with how this is done). Discuss with your instructor about which is the best way to proceed.

_____

_____

_____

_____

_____

_____

_____

_____

_____

_____

_____

_____

_____

_____

_____

_____

_____

_____

_____

_____

You will want to keep in mind any or all of the following points while the group is in session:

- Your comprehensive goal is to manage and maintain a cohesive therapeutic learning environment that provides social skills improvement, support, and individual growth.
- Motivating non-voluntary clients.
- Introduce group members, if necessary.
- Present your agenda to the members, checking for consent on the proposed items.
- Prepare, explain, and discuss the structure of the meeting.
- Use skills to foster understanding of the purpose and goals of the group.
- Use skills to facilitate task accomplishment within the group.
- Respond purposely to questions, comments, and concerns of members.
- Facilitate the group process-using available skill set.
- Develop and implement your plan for ending this group session.

ROLES FOR GROUP MEMBERS

Prior to the beginning of the group, student group members, with the assistance of the instructor, will get themselves "centered" if necessary, so that they may be able to engage in role playing as members of the African Americans living with HIV/AIDS group that is concerned with promoting the support and growth of individual members.

1) **Before you start**, get together with the other members to choose which role you will be playing during this exercise. You will want to develop the identity and story of the member you will play prior to the group exercise. To help you become more acquainted with your role, develop a **character profile** about the person you are playing, describing the character, issues, concerns, and willingness to participate in the group.

As you develop your character, we encourage you to ensure diversity is present in all its many forms within the group. As you consider who you will be and your concerns, consider whether or not you will represent an oppressed group. Will you be someone that is differently-abled, someone that is practicing a non-traditional faith or is an atheist, or perhaps lives in poverty and/or without health insurance? **Please consult your instructor as you develop your character prior to the group exercise.**

Character: _____

_____

_____

_____

_____

_____

_____

_____

_____

_____

_____

You will also want to function in a genuine manner while the group is in session. For instance, if you are unclear about something the facilitator(s) say, then you should express yourself honestly and seek clarity.

OBSERVER TASKS

The remaining students in the class are "**observers-only**" during the group process and should sit quietly around the perimeter of the group. Observers will be assessing the performance of the group facilitators and at a later time will share their professional observations with other group exercise participants.

1) Use the following chart to help with your expectations and observations. Here are some questions to get you started: "What do you expect will happen during this group?" "What do you expect to see the facilitators doing?" "Which social work knowledge, values, and skills do you expect to be present in this educational/support group meeting?" "Are there concepts of group practice that you think will be particularly helpful to the facilitators as they conduct their work?"

Expectations Before the Group Session	Observations During the Group Session
Knowledge:	Knowledge:
Skills:	Skills:
Values:	Values:
Other:	Other:

REFLECTING ON THE GROUP SESSION

A critical portion of this learning exercise is the processing that takes place immediately after the exercise. At the end of the group, all students will have the opportunity to participate in a post-group reflection exercise. The purpose of this reflection is to process the experiences of the group session and to understand the meaning of what transpired.

This process typically begins with the student group facilitators describing their experience leading the group. **Group facilitators**: you are expected to share the thoughts and emotions that you experienced during the group. Most importantly, you will provide a critique of your work that includes a **balanced assessment** of your strengths and areas for improvement. Then, each participating group member, including the joker(s), should use the "round robin" technique to provide balanced feedback for the facilitators. Lastly, the observers will comment on the exercise.

All members of the class (facilitators, group members, observers, and jokers) should consider the knowledge, skills and values that were demonstrated during the group exercise. In addition, feedback and reflection upon what was absent during the experience that perhaps could have assisted with group progress will make for meaningful group discussion. We hope

that during this reflection exercise   you are able to consider your own skills and the skills of your colleagues in context with what you've learned thus far in your curriculum and in this course in particular.

SUMMARY, KEY CONCEPTS, AND PRINCIPLES

You have just had the unique experience of participating in a support/growth/social skills group for African Americans living with HIV/AIDS. Hopefully, this exercise was interesting and contributed to your understanding of the complexities of group work. As you take time to reflect on the session and the social work knowledge, skills, and values that were manifested in the experience, you might consider any one or more of the following key concepts and principles:

Systems Theory	Cohesion
Multicultural Perspective	Cultural Diversity
Strengths Perspective	Stages of Grieving
Feminist Theory	Process Model for Change
Queer Theory	Power presence within the group
Conflict Theory	NASW Code of Ethics
Group norms and roles	Spirituality
Structure	

WEB RESOURCES

AIDS National Interfaith Network
http://www.aidsfaith.com/resource.asp
 Provides info on HIV/AIDS activities for more than 1200 religious organizations.

AIDS Resource Foundation for Children
http://www.aidsresource.org
Provides cost-effective, family-centered services to children coping with the impact of HIV/AIDS.

Centers for Disease Control AIDS Clearinghouse
http://www.cdc.gov/hiv
 National resource center on the latest HIV/AIDS news, policies, publications, and research.

Family AIDS Network (FAN)
http://www.marrrigg.org/w/aids.aspx
FAN is a program that helps the needs of HIV positive children and their families who are infected and/or affected by HIV/AIDS.

National Association of People with AIDS (NAPWA)
http://www.napwa.org/
NAPWA is the oldest and the first National AIDS

organization. This organization is the trusted and independent voice of people living with HIV. It provides information and resources about HIV through referrals, health promotion campaigns, and capacity building and training. NAPWA remains a strong voice in policy, leadership development, capacity building, and social networking for over 25 years.

National Minority AIDS Council
http://www.nmac.org
Develops leadership in communities of color to address the challenges of HIV/AIDS.

National Native American Aids Prevention Center
http://www.nnapc.org
NNAAPC helps organizations that serve Native communities to plan develop and manage HIV/AIDS prevention, intervention care, and treatment programs. NNAAPC addresses the impact of HIV/AIDS on American Indians, Alaskan Natives, and Native Hawaiians through culturally appropriate advocacy, research, education, and policy development in support of healthy indigenous people.

National Women's Health Network

http://www.nwhn.org

The National Women's Health Network improves the health of all women by developing and promoting a critical analysis of health issues in order to affect policy and consumer decision making. The Network aspires to a health care system that is guided by social justice and reflects the needs of diverse women.

Black AIDS Institute

http://www.blackaids.org

The Black AIDS Institute is the first Black HIV/AIDS policy center dedicated to reducing HIV/AIDS health disparities by mobilizing Black Institutions and individuals in efforts to confront the epidemic in their communities.

The AIDS Institute

http://www.theaidsinstitute.org

The AIDS Institutive promotes action for social change though policy research, advocacy, and community education.

Gay Men's Health Crisis of New York (GMHC)

http://www.gmhc.org

An organization founded in 1981, GMHC offers hands on support services in New York City and education, and advocacy for hundreds of thousands nationwide.

CHAPTER 5

A GROUP PRACTICE EXERCISE WITH

VETERANS WITH
POST TRAUMATIC STRESS DISORDER (PTSD)

JULIE UNDERWOOD, STEPHEN ERICH
& HEATHER KANENBERG

By the end of this exercise, you should be able to demonstrate:

- Knowledge of the unique dynamics associated with an open support group

- Knowledge of the bio/psycho/social/spiritual consequences combat exposure may have on returning war veterans

- An awareness of the causal factors, symptoms, and evidence- based treatments associated with PTSD.

- Evidence of competence in dealing with culturally diverse groups

BEFORE YOU BEGIN

The purpose of this exercise is to introduce students to group practice issues and experiences when working with veterans diagnosed with Post Traumatic Stress Disorder (PTSD). It will be important that you take time both in and out of class to prepare for such a task. It is expected that you will have been exposed to theory and information related to veterans and Post Traumatic Stress Disorder.

Some background information to aid in your preparation: The need for such groups has escalated over the past few years as a consequence of the war on terror. Sadly, many men and women are returning from active duty only to discover that the real battle has just begun. In addition to the debilitating symptoms and behaviors which hinder their well-being, some must also struggle with a system that refuses to support them. In 2008, veteran action groups such as Citizens for Responsibility and Ethics in Washington, and VoteVets.org reacted to an internal memo distributed to staff within the Department of Veterans Affairs that encouraged mental health specialist and social workers to reduce the number of PTSD diagnosis given. This meant that many soldiers who should have been given a PTSD diagnosis were instead diagnosed with adjustment disorder, a less severe reaction to stress. This was done in an effort to minimize benefits and services available to ailing soldiers (VoteVet.org, 2008).

If you don't consider yourself familiar with this information or prepared for the exercise, you'll need to review some of this essential content in order to aid in your effectiveness. Feel free to use the web resources at the end of the exercise, the initial chapters of the book, the bibliography at the end of the text, your other textbooks, and also your instructor as resources to help you prepare.

GROUP EXERCISE:
VETERANS WITH POST TRAUMATIC STRESS DISORDER (PTSD)

You and your co-leader have been selected to facilitate the Support Group for Veterans with PTSD at a local non-profit organization (typically 45 minutes – 1 hour).

SCENARIO

Two students will facilitate an open support group for veterans diagnosed with PTSD. Participants will be at different stages of intervention. meaning the group leaders will be expected to have the knowledge and skills necessary to facilitate the individual stage of treatment for each client. The purpose of this group is to learn how to cope with the trauma experienced during war, and provide social support from others who have had similar experiences and to help members change behaviors.

The sponsoring agency for this particular group is a nonprofit organization that offers individual, family, group and community services nationally. As this is an open group, it is understood that participants will be at different stages of treatment/intervention. Members may opt out of the group at anytime though completion of the program is strongly recommended.

Typically, each participant will engage in 1 hour sessions weekly for the duration of 12 -16 weeks. The support group will consist of 8 clients. As participants terminate, replacements will be taken from an agency waiting list in the order they were received. All group participants must be veterans from the wars in Iraq and Afghanistan who are not receiving professional services for PTSD outside of the group and currently do not meet criteria for PTSD and substance abuse comorbidity.

GROUP FACILITATOR TASKS

You and a co-leader are MSW/BSW students leading a therapeutic open group for veterans diagnosed with PTSD as a result of combat exposure. It is understood that this is an ongoing group and members will be at different stages of intervention. Once introductions of any new members have been made and confidentiality, group rules, procedures and roles have been discussed, you will begin the therapeutic process.

1) To begin, you and your co-facilitator will want to conduct some research to develop your identity and some context for this role. *See the Character Profile assignment in Group Member Section.*

2) Ensure that during your group you ask people to report on their status compared to last week (during the introductions, check-in, etc.).

3) Prior to the group, you will need to develop an agenda for your group meeting. Jot down some ideas of what you will need to include in your agenda. Feel free to use the following space to develop your agenda with your co-leader. If you need some assistance, review the 'Before you Begin' and 'Scenario' portions of the exercise. You can also use the sample agendas in Appendix 1 as a guide. You will need to make the agenda available to your members in some way. You can post the agenda or distribute a copy of it to each participant on the day of the exercise (feel free to be creative with how this is done). Talk with your instructor about which is the best way to proceed.

_____

_____

_____

_____

_____

_____

_____

_____

_____

_____

_____

_____

_____

_____

_____

_____

_____

_____

_____

_____

You will want to keep in mind any or all of the following points while the group is in session:
- Create an environment conducive to healthy communication and understanding.
- Introduce group members, if necessary.
- Present your agenda to the members in some form, checking for consent on the proposed items.
- Prepare, explain, and discuss the structure of the meeting.
- Use skills to foster understanding of the purpose and goals of the group.
- Use skills to facilitate task accomplishment within the group.
- Respond purposely to questions, comments, and concerns of members.
- Facilitate the group process-using available skill set.
- Develop and implement your plan for ending this group session.

ROLES FOR GROUP MEMBERS

Prior to the beginning of the group, you, with the assistance of your instructor, will get yourself "centered," if necessary, so that you will be able to engage in role playing as members of the Support Group for Veterans experiencing PTSD.

1) In this exercise, there are several participants but no identified roles or character descriptions for them. Before you start, get together with the other members to identify your role and character. You will want to assume the identity and story of the member you choose prior to the group exercise. To help you become more acquainted with your role, develop a **character profile** about the person you are playing, describing her/his character, age and "story," how they came to be members in the PTSD group, and her/his current status in the group.

As you develop your character, we encourage you to ensure diversity is present in all its many forms within the group. As you consider who you will be and your concerns, consider whether or not you will represent an oppressed group. Are you a veteran that experienced a physical injury while at war? Perhaps you are a member of a low-income family or have recently become homeless? **Please consult your instructor as you develop your character prior to the group exercise.**

Character: _____

_____

_____

_____

_____

_____

_____

_____

_____

_____

_____

You will also want to function in a genuine manner while the group is in session. For instance, if you are unclear about something the facilitator(s) say, then you should express yourself honestly and seek clarity.

OBSERVER TASKS

Your role for this exercise is that of an **observer**. You have had or will have a chance to facilitate or participate in an exercise in your class, but during this group process experience you should sit quietly around the perimeter of the group. You will be assessing the performance of the group facilitators and at a later time will share your professional observations with other group exercise participants.

1) Use the following chart to help with your expectations and observations. Here are some questions to get you started: 'What do you expect will take place during this group?'""What do you expect to see the facilitators doing?""Which social work knowledge, values, and skills do you expect to be present in this Veterans support meeting?" "Are there concepts of group practice that you think will be particularly helpful to the facilitators as they conduct their work?"

Expectations Before the Group Session	Observations During the Group Session
Knowledge:	Knowledge:
Skills:	Skills:
Values:	Values:
Other:	Other:

REFLECTING ON THE GROUP SESSION

A critical portion of this learning exercise is the processing that takes place immediately after the exercise. At the end of the group, all students will have the opportunity to participate in a post-group reflection exercise. The purpose of this reflection is to process the experiences of the group session and to make meaning of what transpired.

This process typically begins with the student group facilitators describing their experience leading the group. **Group facilitators**: you are expected to share the thoughts and emotions that you experienced during the group. Most importantly, you will provide a critique of your work that includes a **balanced assessment** of your strengths and areas for improvement. Then, each **participating group member**, including the joker(s), should use the "round robin" technique to provide balanced feedback for the facilitators. Lastly, the **observers** will comment on the exercise.

All members of the class (facilitators, group members, observers, and jokers) should consider the knowledge, skills and values that were demonstrated during the group exercise. In addition, feedback and reflection upon what was absent during the experience that perhaps could have assisted with group progress will make for meaningful group discussion. Our hope for you during this reflection exercise is that you are able to consider your own skills and the skills of your colleagues in context with what you've learned thus far in your curriculum and in this course in particular.

SUMMARY, KEY CONCEPTS, AND PRINCIPLES

You have just had the unique experience of participating in a support group for service members experiencing Post Traumatic Stress Disorder and dealing with the impact of war on their lives. Hopefully this exercise was interesting and contributed to your understanding of the complexities of group work. As you take time to reflect on the session and the social work knowledge, skills, and values that were manifested in the experience, you might consider any one or more of the following key concepts and principles:

Ecological theory
Systems theory
Multicultural perspectives
Strengths perspectives
Feminist theory
Queer theory
Conflict theories

Cognitive development
Identity development
Attachment Theory
Grief and Loss dynamics by adolescent
Cognitive/Behavioral
Psychodynamic
Humanist Theory
Gestalt Based Trauma Theory

WEB RESOURCES

National Center for PTSD
http://www.ncptsd.va.gov/ncmain/index.jsp
This website, created by the Department of Veteran Affairs, educates healthcare providers and the public in general about the causes, symptoms and treatment of PTSD. Additionally, students will find up to date research concerning PTSD, assessment tools, and an online resource center for a multitude of PTSD related topics.

NAMI Veterans Resource Center
http://www.nami.org/Template.cfm?Section=PTSD&Template=/TaggedPage/TaggedPageDisplay.cfm&TPLID=86&ContentID=52905
This resource provides veterans and their families with information about the causes, symptoms and treatments of PTSD. The website also offers online discussion boards, current news, and media coverage of related topics.

Iraq War Veterans Organization, Inc.
http://www.iraqwarveterans.org/index.html
The Iraq War Veterans Organization was designed to address the needs, educate and support veterans from the war in Iraq and their families. There are links to online support groups, education and work opportu-

nities as well as deployment information. There is also a section dedicated to PTSD

Veteran's Legislation
http://www.va.gov/oca/vet_legis.asp
This website, also created by the Department of Veterans Affairs, conveniently links its users to recent legislation concerning veterans.

Citizens for Responsibility and Ethics in Washington (CREW)
http://www.citizensforethics.org/
CREW is a group dedicated to monitoring the actions of our government and holding elected officials responsible for unethical behavior. This website has exhaustive reports and lawsuits concerning decisions affecting veterans.

VoteVets.org
http://www.votevets.org/index_html
VoteVets.org is a political action committee devoted to keeping the needs of veteran's in the political eye. This website includes information on current campaigns as well as hot topics and news about macro level issues affecting our veterans.

CHAPTER 6

A GROUP PRACTICE EXERCISE WITH

YOUNGER AND OLDER ADOLESCENTS IN RESIDENTIAL TREATMENT

SHARON K. HALL & STEPHEN ERICH

By the end of this exercise, you should be able to demonstrate:

- Knowledge regarding common DSM diagnoses in adolescence that could result in admission to residential treatment facilities.

- Knowledge of milieu therapy in residential treatment facilities.

- Knowledge of the strengths and weaknesses associated with adolescent inpatient treatment.

- Knowledge of developmental differences between younger and older adolescents.

- Evidence of competence related to the use of group work skills via the in-class group facilitation exercise (ex: testing, modeling, conflict, etc.).

BEFORE YOU BEGIN

The purpose of this module is to introduce you and your peers to group practice issues and experiences when working with younger (12-15) and older (16-19) adolescents residing in a residential treatment facility. It will be important that you take time both in and out of class to prepare for such a task. It is expected that you will have been exposed to theory and information related to adolescent development and residential treatment.

Some background information to aid in your preparation: Research suggests that younger and older adolescents differ in many developmental ways, often resulting in different problem-solving strategies. Moreover, their view of the self and of others continues to develop throughout the adolescent years, increasing the challenges for professionals who intervene with them. **BSW and MSW trained professionals may lead or co-facilitate treatment groups that are often named "Community Groups" in residential treatment facilities.** The purpose of these groups may vary somewhat from setting to setting, but they frequently involve the development of mutual support, as well as age appropriate social skills, such as taking turns, identifying and differentiating between thoughts, feelings, and behaviors and conflict resolution. Work in community groups is widely considered one piece of a comprehensive treatment plan that may also include individual and family therapy and medications as appropriate. A treatment team is typically responsible for devising and implementing the treatment plan. A treatment team may include one or more of the following disciplines: social worker, physician/psychiatrist, psychologist, couple and family therapist, nurse and paraprofessionals. Often times, adolescents in these types of treatment facilities must progress through a level system by achieving progressively more mature behavioral expectations for each level. It is not uncommon for adolescents in these treatment facilities to"drop"one or more levels by exhibiting inappropriate behavior during the course of their treatment.

If you don't consider yourself familiar with this information or prepared for the exercise, you'll need to review some of this essential content in order to aid in your effectiveness. Feel free to use the web resources at the end of the exercise, the initial chapters of the book, the bibliography at the end of the text, your other textbooks, and also your instructor as resources to help you prepare.

GROUP EXERCISE:
YOUNGER AND OLDER ADOLESCENTS
IN RESIDENTIAL TREATMENT

You and your co-leader have been selected to facilitate the"community group"for adolescents in your residential treatment facility (typically 45 minutes – 1 hour).

SCENARIO

The adolescent unit at Pleasantville Residential Treatment Center serves adolescents who have any of the following DSM-IV-R Diagnostic conditions: Mood disorders; behavior disorders, substance abuse disorders, etc. The role of the psyc tech is to be with the adolescents on the unit and facilitate their movement through their daily schedules. Tech's supervise and assist with meals, schoolwork, free time, and various support group activities, including the daily community group. **The purpose of the community group** is for individual members to discuss issues related to their treatment, emotional/behavioral status, to give feedback (supportive or confrontive) to their peers, as well as to address unit "group" issues. The type and quality of interactional processes that occur in the community group represent, in part, the therapeutic milieu. These groups typically have some adolescents who are at any or all stages of their treatment while also representing different developmental stages (younger/older). Thus, some members are more experienced leaders to newer members in the group. The group is open to new members, ongoing and lasts for about 45 minutes on most occasions. Today, one of the adolescents is leaving the facility. She has progressed rather quickly to the second highest level in the unit level system, suggesting her behavior and work in therapy is progressing nicely. She is requesting feedback from the "community" regarding her readiness for discharge into outpatient treatment. As group facilitators, your goal is to guide the group participants so that they reach an acceptable level of closure for the meeting.

GROUP FACILITATOR TASKS

You and your co-leader are working on a psychiatric unit as paraprofessionals (psyc techs). You are leading a "community group" on the adolescent unit of the Pleasantville Residential Treatment Center.

1) To begin, you and your co-facilitator will want to conduct some research to develop your identity and some context for this role. *See Character Profile assignment in the Group Member Section.*

2) Prior to the group, you will need to develop an agenda for your group meeting. Jot down some ideas of what you will need to include in your agenda. Feel free to use the following space to develop your agenda with your co-leader. If you need some assistance, review the "Before you Begin" and "Scenario" portions of the exercise. You can also use the sample agendas in Appendix 1 as a guide. You will need to make the agenda available to your members in some way. You can post the agenda or distribute a copy of it to each participant on the day of the exercise (feel free to be creative with how this is done). Talk with your instructor about which is the best way to proceed.

_____

_____

_____

_____

_____

_____

_____

_____

_____

_____

_____

_____

_____

_____

_____

_____

_____

_____

_____

You will want to keep in mind any or all of the following points while the group is in session:

- Create an environment conducive to healthy communication and understanding.
- Introduce group members, if necessary.
- Present your agenda to the members in some form, checking for agreement on the proposed items.
- Prepare, explain, and discuss the structure of the meeting.
- Use skills to foster understanding of the purpose and goals of the group.
- Use skills to facilitate task accomplishment within the group.
- Respond purposely to questions, comments, and concerns of members.
- Facilitate the group process-using available skill set.
- Develop and implement your plan for ending this group session.

ROLES FOR GROUP MEMBERS

Prior to the beginning of the group, you, with the assistance of your instructor, will get yourself "centered," if necessary, so that you will be able to engage in role playing as members of the Community Group that are concerned with their treatment progress, status (emotional, behavioral, programmatic, etc.) and the unit functioning.

1) In this exercise, there are several participants but no identified roles or character descriptions for them. **Before you start**, get together with the other members to identify your role and character. Keep in mind there are some expectations that some members will be younger adolescents and some will be older adolescents. You will want to be sure this is

present among all participants as you and your classmates <u>select your role</u> and <u>develop your identity.</u> You will want to assume the identity and story of the member you choose prior to the group exercise. To help you become more acquainted with your role, develop a **character profile** about the person you are playing, describing the character, <u>her/his age</u> and "<u>story,</u>" how she/he come to the <u>inpatient unit,</u> and <u>her/his status in the group.</u>

As you develop your character, we encourage you to ensure diversity is present in all its many forms within the group. As you consider who you will be and your concerns, consider whether or not you will <u>represent an oppressed group.</u> You'll want to ensure that there are adolescents in the group that represent diversity in race and ethnicity, age, sexual orientation/gender identity, religion, physical ability, and more. **Please consult your instructor as you develop your character prior to the group exercise.**

Character: _____

_____

_____

_____

_____

_____

_____

_____

_____

_____

_____

_____

_____

You will also want to behave in a genuine manner while the group is in session. For instance, if you are unclear about something the facilitator(s) say, then you should express yourself honestly and seek clarity.

OBSERVER TASKS

Your role for this exercise is that of an **observer**. You have had or will have a chance to facilitate or participate in an exercise in your class, but during this group process experience you should sit quietly around the perimeter of the group. You will be assessing the performance of the group facilitators and at a later time will share your professional observations with other group exercise participants.

1) Use the following chart to help with your expectations and observations. Here are some questions to get you started: "What do you expect will take place during this group?" "What do you expect to see the facilitators doing?" "Which social work knowledge, values, and skills do you expect to be present in this 'community' group meeting?" "Are there concepts of group practice that you think will be particularly helpful to the facilitators as they conduct their work?"

Expectations Before the Group Session	Observations During the Group Session
Knowledge:	Knowledge:
Skills:	Skills:
Values:	Values:
Other:	Other:

REFLECTING ON THE GROUP SESSION

A critical portion of this learning exercise is the processing that takes place immediately after the exercise. At the end of the group, all students will have the opportunity to participate in a post-group reflection exercise. The purpose of this reflection is to process the experiences of the group session and to understand the meaning of what transpired.

This process typically begins with the student group facilitators describing their experience leading the group. **Group facilitators**: you are expected to share the thoughts and emotions that you experienced during the group. Most importantly, you will provide a critique of your work that includes a **balanced assessment** of your strengths and areas for improvement. Then, each **participating group member**, including the joker(s), should use the "round robin" technique to provide balanced feedback for the facilitators. Lastly, the **observers** will comment on the exercise.

All members of the class (facilitators, group members, observers, and jokers) should consider the knowledge, skills, and values that were demonstrated during the group exercise. In addition, feedback and reflection upon what was absent during the experience that perhaps could have assisted with group progress will make for meaningful group discussion. We hope that during this reflection exercise   you are able to consider your own skills and the skills of your colleagues in context with what you've learned thus far in your curriculum and in this course in particular.

SUMMARY, KEY CONCEPTS, AND PRINCIPLES

You have just had the unique experience of participating in a Community Group for younger and older adolescents in a residential treatment facility. Hopefully this exercise was interesting and contributed to your understanding of the complexities of group work. As you take time to reflect on the session and the social work knowledge, skills, and values that were manifested in the experience, you might consider any one or more of the following key concepts and principles:

Ecological theory
Systems theory
Multicultural perspectives
Strengths perspectives
Feminist theory
Queer theory
Conflict theories
Cognitive development

Identity development
Attachment Theory
Grief and Loss dynamics by adolescent
    developmental period (younger/older)
Cognitive/Behavioral Theory
Psychodynamic Theory
Humanist Theory

WEB RESOURCES

Youth Communication: True stories by teens.
www.youthcomm.org.
This site has short books written by adolescents about various challenges and social/cultural background issues in the U.S.

American Psychological Association
www.apa.org.
This is the official site of the American Psychological Association and has links for many adolescent disorders and treatment options.

National Clearinghouse of Alcohol and Drug Information
www.health.org.
This site is a Federal site that has links to adolescent mental health needs and treatment.

The Annie E. Casey Foundation
www.aecf.org
This is the official site of the Annie E. Casey Foundation that serves children, youth and families by providing data and treatment option summaries for adolescents at risk for various mental health problems.

Youth Care, Inc.
http://www.youthcare.com/
Youth Care is a licensed residential treatment center for adolescents ages 11-18. While at Youth Care, your pre-teen or teenager will receive intensive therapeutic services from caring, experienced therapists who only want to see your child succeed

SECTION 3

CLOSED AND TIME LIMITED TREATMENT GROUPS

CHAPTER 7

A GROUP PRACTICE EXERCISE WITH

SINGLE MOTHERS WHO HAVE EXPERIENCED EPISODIC HOMELESSNESS

RHONDA HARVEY, BSW, STEPHEN ERICH, PH.D, LCSW
& HEATHER KANENBERG, PH.D, LMSW

By the end of this exercise, you should be able to demonstrate the application of:

- Theoretical knowledge of group functioning
- Theoretical knowledge of the issues surrounding homelessness
- Cultural competency
- Appropriate usage of terminology
- Group work skills especially those specific to the "end stage" of group development

BEFORE YOU BEGIN

The purpose of this course exercise is to introduce students to group practice issues and experiences when working with mothers that have experienced episodic homelessness. It will be important that you take time both in and out of class to prepare for such a task.

As a bit of background to aid in your preparation: This course module assumes students will have been exposed to essential theoretical content, including theory specifically related to women and homelessness, systemic oppression, employment discrimination, social stigma, basic needs issues, child care and development, and more. You are also expected to be familiar with language appropriate for working with this community as well as theory and skills relevant to the facilitation of support and educational groups. This chapter, as described here, is a one or two-class period process depending on whether theoretical content is presented in the current class or a previous one. Your instructor may modify this exercise so that it best meet your needs.

If you don't consider yourself familiar with this information or prepared for the exercise, you'll need to review some of this essential content in order to aid in your effectiveness. Feel free to use the web resources at the end of the exercise, the initial chapters of the book, the bibliography at the end of the text, your other textbooks, and also your instructor as resources to help you prepare.

GROUP EXERCISE:
SINGLE MOTHERS WHO HAVE EXPERIENCED
EPISODIC HOMELESSNESS

You and one of your peers will facilitate a support/education group for a portion of the class period (typically 45-60 minutes).

SCENARIO

This exercise requires two students to act as the co-leaders of a support/educational group for single mothers who have experienced periods of homelessness. The group was developed as part of an aftercare program associated with an urban area women's shelter. Each one of the group members has been a resident of the shelter and has recently transitioned into a more stable living environment. The purpose of this group is to assist in the development of self-sufficiency and provide a supportive network for single mothers. Additional issues for this population can also include family dynamics, obstacles in securing employment, lack of education, health concerns pertaining to themselves and/or their children and childcare. The themes that frequently emerge during group discussion are inadequate income, parenting dilemmas, custody rights, and interpersonal struggles.

Each session is divided into two parts. The first segment is utilized for educational purposes. The leaders are responsible for designing a program activity that emphasizes independent problem solving, building upon previously mastered communication skills. The second segment is reserved for discussion and support. For this meeting, leaders will initiate a conversation about the impending termination of the group.

All participants are aware that this is a closed group which has been meeting for one hour, twice a month, for 5 months thus far. This session is the tenth of twelve. Each woman, along with her children, now resides in a nearby low-income housing area. The shelter is the sponsoring agency and location for the meetings. Group members have engaged in a high level of self-disclosure, resulting in strong cohesion. Diversity within the group is prevalent, as it is dominated by persons of color. All women range in age from 26 to 35.

GROUP FACILITATOR TASKS

You and your co-leader are BSWs leading a support/educational group for single mothers who have experienced homelessness.

1) To begin, you and your co-facilitator will want to conduct some research to develop your identity and some context for this role. *See the Character Profile assignment in Group Member Section.*

2) Prior to the group, you will need to develop an agenda for your group meeting. Jot down some ideas of what you will need to include in your agenda. If you need some assistance, you can use the sample agendas in Appendix 1 as a guide. You will need to post the agenda or distribute a copy of it to each participant on the day of the exercise. Talk with your instructor about which is best.

_____

_____

_____

_____

_____

_____

_____

_____

_____

_____

_____

_____

_____

_____

_____

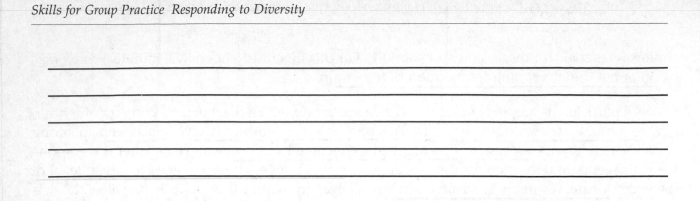

You will want to keep in mind all or many of the following while the group is in session:

- Create an environment conducive to healthy communication and understanding.
- Introduce group members, if necessary.
- Cover/review confidentiality and group rules, procedures, and roles, if necessary.
- Prepare, explain, and discuss the structure of today's meeting and the impending termination of the group. (See the chart on page 12 for more information Termination)
- Use skills to foster understanding of the purpose and goals of the group.
- Respond purposely to questions, comments, and concerns of members.
- Facilitate the group process-using available skill set.
- Develop and implement your plan for ending this group session.

ROLES FOR GROUP MEMBERS

Prior to the beginning of the group, you, with the assistance of your instructor, will get yourself "centered," if necessary, so that you will be able to engage in role playing as members of the single mothers who have experienced homelessness group. Your supportive function is to assume the role of a single mother who has experienced homelessness and is working to maintain her family and newly acquired home.

1) In this exercise, there are several participants but no identified roles or character descriptions for them. **Before you start**, get together with the other members to identify your role and character. Keep in mind there is some guidance about the racial/ethnic make-up of the group in the scenario. You will want to be sure this is present among all participants as you and your classmates select your role and develop your identity. You will want to assume the identity and story of the member you choose prior to the group exercise. To help you become more acquainted with your role, develop a **character profile** about the person you are playing, describing the character, your own personal history, sexual orientation, mental health, and I.Q., which will affect your demeanor and behavior throughout the exercise.

As you develop your character, we encourage you to ensure diversity is present in all its many forms within the group. Do you have a child with chronic health needs or are you engaging in criminal activity? **Please consult your instructor as you develop your character prior to the group exercise.**

Character: _____

_____

_____

_____

_____

_____

_____

_____

_____

_____

_____

You will also want to function in a genuine manner while the group is in session. For instance, if you are unclear about something the facilitator(s) say, then you should express yourself honestly and seek clarity.

OBSERVER TASKS

Your role for this exercise is that of an **observer**. You have had or will have a chance to facilitate or participate in an exercise in your class, but during this group process experience you should sit quietly around the perimeter of the group. You will be assessing the performance of the group facilitators and at a later time will share your professional observations with other group exercise participants.

1) Use the following chart to help with your expectations and observations. Here are some questions to get you started: "What do you expect will happen during this group?" "What do you expect to see the facilitators doing?" "Which social work knowledge, values, and skills do you expect to be present in this group for mothers who have experienced homelessness?" "Are there concepts of group practice that you think will be particularly helpful to the facilitators as they conduct their work?"

Expectations Before the Group Session	Observations During the Group Session
Knowledge:	Knowledge:
Skills:	Skills:
Values:	Values:
Other:	Other:

REFLECTING ON THE GROUP SESSION

A critical portion of this learning exercise is the processing that takes place immediately after the exercise. At the end of the group, all students will have the opportunity to participate in a post-group reflection exercise. The purpose of this reflection is to process the experiences of the group session and to understand the meaning of what transpired.

This process typically begins with the student group facilitators describing their experience leading the group. **Group facilitators**; you are expected to share the thoughts and emotions that you experienced during the group. Most importantly, you will provide a critique of your work that includes a **balanced assessment** of your strengths and areas for improvement. Then, each **participating group member**, including the joker(s), should use the 'round robin' technique to provide balanced feedback for the facilitators. Lastly, the **observers** will comment on the exercise.

All members of the class (facilitators, group members, observers, and jokers) should consider the knowledge, skills and values that were demonstrated during the group exercise. In addition, feedback and reflection upon what was absent during the experience that perhaps could have assisted with group progress will make for meaningful group discussion. Our hope for you during this reflection exercise is that you are able to consider your own skills and the skills of your colleagues in context with what you've learned thus far in your curriculum and in this course in particular.

SUMMARY, KEY CONCEPTS, AND PRINCIPLES

You have just had the unique experience of participating in a support/educational group for mothers who have experienced homelessness. Hopefully this exercise was interesting and contributed to your understanding of the complexities of group work. As you take time to reflect on the session and the social work knowledge, skills, and values that were manifested in the experience, you might consider any one or more of the following key concepts and principles:

Ecological Theory
Systems Theory
Multicultural perspectives
Strengths Perspective
Feminist Theory
Queer Theory
Conflict Theory
Teen Pregnancy

Parents with Mental Illness
Erickson's Psychosocial Stage of
    Development – Young Adulthood
Psychodynamic Theory
Cognitive/Behavioral Theory
Learning Theory
Homelessness: characteristics, causes,
    and helpful interventions

WEB RESOURCES

U.S. Department of Housing and Urban Development
http://www.hud.gov/homeless/index.cfm
Homelessness is a problem that affects many people in America. If you are homeless yourself and need help or if you want to learn more about homelessness and how you can help, we have information for you.

National Alliance to End Homelessness
www.endhomelessness.org
The National Alliance to End Homelessness is a non-

profit, non-partisan, organization committed to preventing and ending homelessness in the United States.

National Coalition for the Homeless
www.nationalhomeless.org
The National Coalition for the Homeless is a national network of people who are currently experiencing or who have experienced homelessness, activists and advocates, community-based and faith-based service providers, and others committed to a single mission.

CHAPTER 8

A GROUP PRACTICE EXERCISE WITH

BI–RACIAL COUPLES

MARILYN SCOTT, STEPHEN ERICH
& HEATHER KANENBERG

By the end of this exercise, you should be able to demonstrate:

- Time limited and closed group skills (particularly with couples).

- Relevant theoretical knowledge of issues related to culture, ethnicity, race, etc. and their relationships with one another.

- An understanding of identity and racial identity development of persons with bi-racial backgrounds.

- The use of appropriate terminology regarding bi-racial identities, culture, ethnicity, race, etc.

- Understanding of NASW issues and ethics pertaining to different cultures.

BEFORE YOU BEGIN

The purposes of this group are to support the development of a positive identity and self-esteem among bi–racial couples and to develop an awareness and acceptance of cultural differences. It will be important that you take time both in and out of class to prepare for such a task. It is expected that you will have been exposed to theory and information related to bi–racial couple relationships and power dynamics in families.

If you don't consider yourself familiar with this information or prepared for the exercise, you'll need to review some of this essential content in order to aid in your effectiveness. Feel free to use the web resources at the end of the exercise, the initial chapters of the book, the bibliography at the end of the text, your other textbooks, and also your instructor as resources to help you prepare.

GROUP EXERCISE:
BI–RACIAL COUPLES

You and your co-leader are facilitating a group for bi–racial couples. The following provides guidance about facilitating the exercise.

SCENARIO

This group is considered to be a closed and time limited group, meaning only the participants who begin the group will complete the group, with no new members added. This is the third of six scheduled meetings with group members. Informed consent issues including confidentiality and group rules have been discussed previously. You as a group leader, should be aware of how the needs, wants, and desires of the person representing the dominate culture within the relationship may take precedence over the needs, wants, and desires of the person representing the secondary or non-dominant culture. Common issues that have surfaced in the three weeks of meeting include power struggles relating to couple roles and child rearing, community attitudes towards bi–racial couples, and conflicting relationships with extended family. You and your co-facilitator are ideally from different cultural backgrounds and you'll be facilitating this support/educational group for a 45-60 minute portion of the class session. This group exercise presents an opportunity for bi–racial couples to understand and focus on the impact of cultural differences on the couple relationship.

GROUP FACILITATOR TASKS

You and your co-leader are BSWs leading a support/educational group for bi–racial couples. As student facilitators, you should possess a fundamental knowledge of group work and be familiar with the cultural backgrounds of participating couples.

1) To begin, you and your co-facilitator will want to conduct some research to develop your identity and some context for this role. *See the Character Profile assignment in Group Member Section.*

2) Prior to the group, you will need to develop an agenda (written or otherwise) for your members. Feel free to use the following space to develop your agenda with your co-leader. If you need some assistance, review the "Before you Begin" and "Scenario" portions of the exercise. You can also use the sample agendas in Appendix 1 as a guide. You will need to make the agenda available to your members in some way. You can post the agenda or distribute a copy of it to each participant on the day of the exercise (feel free to be creative with how this is done). Discuss with your instructor about which is the best way to proceed.

_____

_____

_____

_____

_____

_____

_____

_____

_____

_____

_____

_____

_____

_____

_____

_____

_____

_____

You will want to keep in mind any the following points while the group is in session:

- Introduce group members, if necessary.
- Present your agenda to the members in some form, checking for agreement on the proposed items.
- Prepare, explain, and discuss the structure of the meeting.
- Use skills to foster understanding of the purpose and goals of the group.

- Use skills to facilitate task accomplishment within the group.
- Respond purposely to questions, comments, and concerns of members.
- Facilitate the group process using available skill set.
- Develop and implement your plan for ending this group session.

ROLES FOR GROUP MEMBERS

Prior to the beginning of the group, student group members, with the assistance of the instructor, will get themselves "centered" if necessary, so that they may be able to engage in role playing as members of the Bi–racial Couples Group.

1) In this exercise, there are several couples participating but no identified roles or character descriptions for them. **Before you start**, get together with the other members to identify your role and character. You will want to assume your identity and story prior to the group exercise. You will also need to talk with the person that will role-play your partner to ensure you have a shared understanding of your roles, identity, and reasons for being in the group. To help you become more acquainted with your role, develop a **character profile** about the person you are playing, describing the character, her/his age and 'story', how she/he came to the couples group, including her/his concerns, and her/his status in the group.

As you develop your character, we encourage you to ensure diversity is present in all its many forms within the group. As you consider who you will be and your concerns, consider whether or not you will represent an oppressed group. Consider developing an identity that includes representation of persons who are differently-abled, living in poverty, diagnosed with a serious illness, or visually impaired. **Please consult your instructor as you develop your character prior to the group exercise.**

Character: _____

_____

_____

_____

_____

_____

_____

_____

_____

_____

_____

You will also want to behave in a genuine manner while the group is in session. For instance, if you are unclear about something the facilitator(s) say, then you should express yourself honestly and seek clarity.

OBSERVER TASKS

Your role for this exercise is that of an **observer**. You have had or will have a chance to facilitate or participate in an exercise in your class, but during this group process experience you should sit quietly around the perimeter of the group. You will be assessing the performance of the group facilitators and at a later time will share your professional observations with other group exercise participants.

1) Use the following chart to help with your expectations and observations. Here are some questions to get you started: What do you expect to will take place during this group? What do you expect to see the facilitators doing? Which social work knowledge, values, and skills do you expect to be present in this biracial couple's group meeting? Are there concepts of group practice that you think will be particularly helpful to the facilitators as they conduct their work?

Expectations Before the Group Session	Observations During the Group Session
Knowledge:	Knowledge:
Skills:	Skills:
Values:	Values:
Other:	Other:

REFLECTING ON THE GROUP SESSION

A critical portion of this learning exercise is the processing that takes place immediately after the exercise. At the end of the group, all students will have the opportunity to participate in a post-group reflection exercise. The purpose of this reflection is to process the experiences of the group session and to understand the meaning of what transpired.

This process typically begins with the student group facilitators describing their experience leading the group. **Group facilitators**, you are expected to share the thoughts and emotions that you experienced during the group. Most importantly, you will provide a critique of your work that includes a **balanced assessment** of your strengths and areas for improvement. Then, each **participating group member**, including the joker(s), should use the 'round robin' technique to provide balanced feedback for the facilitators. Lastly, the **observers** will comment on the exercise.

All members of the class (facilitators, group members, observers, and jokers) should consider the knowledge, skills and values that were demonstrated during the group exercise. In addition, feedback and reflection upon what was absent during the experience that perhaps could have assisted with group progress will make for meaningful group discussion. We hope that during this reflection exercise you are able to consider your own skills and the skills of your colleagues in context with what you've learned thus far in your curriculum and in this course in particular.

SUMMARY, KEY CONCEPTS, AND PRINCIPLES

You have just had the unique experience of participating in a group for biracial couples. Hopefully this exercise was interesting and contributed to your understanding of the complexities of group work. As you take time to reflect on the session and the social work knowledge, skills, and values that were manifested in the experience, you might consider any one or more of the following key concepts and principles:

Emancipation Theory	Group norms and roles
Multicultural Perspective	Group Cohesion
Strengths Perspective	Cultural Diversity
Ecological Theory	Feminist Theory
Conflict Theory	Queer Theory

WEB RESOURCES

Bi–racial Family Network
http://www.bfnchicago.org/index.html
The Biracial Family Network (BFN) is a nonprofit 501(c)(3) public benefit corporation based in Chicago organized to help eliminate prejudice and discrimination by assisting individuals and families of diverse ethnic ancestry to improve the quality of their intercultural relationships via education and social activities. BFN does not tolerate discrimination based on age, color, nationality, race, religion, or sex.

Association of MultiEthnic Americans (AMEA)
http://www.ameasite.org/
The Association of MultiEthnic Americans (AMEA), a non-profit organization, is an international association of organizations dedicated to advocacy, education and collaboration on behalf of the multiethnic, multiracial and transracial adoption community.

Bi–racial Youth and Families in Therapy: Issues and Interventions (Journal Article)
http://findarticles.com/p/articles/mi_qa3658/is_200007/ai_n8924699/
In this article, a nationally representative database is used to compare functioning in biracial youth to white adolescents and other minority adolescents. Results suggest that biracial/biethnic youth are a particularly vulnerable group in terms of self reported delinquency school problems, internalizing symptoms, and self regard.

Project RACE
http://projectrace.com/
The national organization leading the movement for a multiracial classification.

The Multiracial Activist
http://www.multiracial.com/site/
The Multiracial Activist (TMA) is a libertarian oriented activist journal covering social and civil liberties issues of interest to individuals who perceive themselves to be "biracial" or "multiracial," "interracial" couples/families and "transracial" adoptees.

CHAPTER 9

A GROUP PRACTICE EXERCISE WITH

POST-ADOPTION FAMILY GROUP

STEPHEN ERICH & HEATHER KANENBERG

By the end of this exercise, you should be able to demonstrate:

- Knowledge regarding parents who have adopted children with special needs status through your performance in the in-class group facilitation exercise.

- Knowledge of terminology appropriate for working with this community (special needs status, adoption triad, finalization, birth family, etc.).

- Evidence of competence related to the use of group work skills via the in-class group facilitation exercise.

BEFORE YOU BEGIN

The purpose of this exercise is to introduce students to group practice issues and experiences when working with a diverse group of adoptive families in a unique format designed to address the needs of adoptive parents and their adopted children with special needs. It will be important that you take time both in and out of class to prepare for such a task. It is expected that you will have been exposed to theory and information related to child development, developmental disabilities, mental health issues, grief and loss, and theories of adoption and attachment.

As a bit of background to aid in your preparation: This model of group work involves three phases. The first phase includes all parents and children as well as two facilitators for each group. During the first phase of the group, all parties (parents, children, facilitators) eat a dinner provided by the host agency. On special occasions, the parents volunteer to provide a pot luck dinner for everyone. During this communal "breaking of bread," families and sub-group facilitators greet one another, various stakeholders may make announcements, family members update facilitators about various "issues," and group facilitators engage in last-minute planning for the following phases. At the end of this first phase (approx. 30-45 minutes), the large group separates into four distinct groups, each with two group facilitators: A parent's group, a teen group, a pre-teen (tween) group and a young children's group each of which then go to their identified meeting room. The second phase is composed of these concurrent meetings that last approximately one hour. This allows each family member, in a developmental manner, to discuss and work on issues with other like members of the adoptive family. The third and final phase of this group work model involves the four distinct groups once again matriculating into the original group room for a "wrap-up" with all members of each adoptive family.

The sponsoring agency is a private-not-for-profit entity. Group facilitators are not employed by this agency, but act as "contractors" with the State to provide these services. Sponsorship by the agency includes referrals to the group, advertising, and some "goodies" including paper plates, napkins, etc. for the communal meals. This group is composed of 12 sessions. Each one lasts for about two hours.

If you don't consider yourself familiar with this information or prepared for the exercise, you'll need to review some of this essential content in order to aid in your effectiveness. Feel free to use the web resources at the end of the exercise, the initial chapters of the book, the bibliography at the end of the text, your other textbooks, and also your instructor as resources to help you prepare.

GROUP EXERCISE:
POST-ADOPTION FAMILY GROUP

One or two students will be selected to facilitate a support/education group for a portion of the class period (typically 45-60 minutes).

SCENARIO

You are one or one of two social workers who provide post-adoption family group services to families whose children have special needs. You and your co-leader (optional) are BSWs leading a first meeting of this support/educational/social skills group for families who have finalized the adoption of their child or children (sibling group). **The purpose of this group** is to support the development of healthy attachments among adoptive family members, to help adopted children resolve grief, loss, and trauma issues resulting from neglect and/or abuse in their birth families as well as other prior placements and to promote developmentally appropriate behavior. To this end, group facilitators foster the development of a safe and mutually supportive and educational environment where family members can help each other build and sustain healthy individual and family functioning.

Student group facilitators are expected to have familiarity with issues common to parents who have adopted children with special needs as well as to adopted children at various ages. **Although, the exercise involves only work during the first session and stage two of this model, students should be prepared to address group member's issues in a developmentally appropriate manner**.

GROUP FACILITATOR TASKS

One or two students will be selected to facilitate a support/education group for post adoption families.

1) To begin, you and your co-facilitator will want to conduct some research to develop your identity and some context for this role. *See the Character Profile assignment in Group Member Section.*

2) Prior to the group, you will need to develop an agenda for your group meeting. Jot down some ideas of what you will need to include in your agenda. Feel free to use the following space to develop your agenda with your co-leader. If you need some assistance, review the "Before you Begin" and "Scenario" portions of the exercise. You can also use the sample agendas in Appendix 1 as a guide. You will need to make the agenda available to your members in some way. You can post the agenda or distribute a copy of it to each participant on the day of the exercise (feel free to be creative with how this is done). Talk with your instructor about the best way to proceed.

_____

_____

_____

_____

_____

_____

_____

_____

_____

_____

_____

_____

_____

_____

_____

_____

_____

_____

_____

_____

You will want to keep in mind any or all of the following points while the group is in session:

- Create an environment conducive to healthy communication and understanding.
- Introduce group members, if necessary.
- Cover confidentiality and group rules, procedures, and roles, if necessary.
- Present your agenda to the members in some form, checking for agreement on the proposed items.
- Prepare, explain, and discuss the structure of the meeting.
- Use skills to foster understanding of the purpose and goals of the group.
- Use skills to facilitate task accomplishment within the group.
- Respond purposely to questions, comments, and concerns of members.
- Facilitate the group process-using available skill set.
- Develop and implement your plan for ending this group session.

ROLES FOR GROUP MEMBERS

Prior to the beginning of the group, you, with the assistance of your instructor, will get yourself "centered," if necessary, so that you will be able to engage in role playing as members of the Adoption Family Group concerned with developing healthy attachment among families and adoptee's.

1) In this exercise, there are several participants but no identified roles or character descriptions for them. **Before you start**, get together with the other members to identify your role

and character. You will want to assume the identity and story of the member you decide to role-play prior to the group exercise. To help you become more acquainted with your role, develop a **character profile** about the person you are playing, describing her/his character, age information, partnership, and how the couple came to adopt from this agency.

As you develop your character, we encourage you to ensure diversity is present in all its many forms within the group. As you consider who you will be and your concerns, consider whether or not you will represent an oppressed group. Perhaps you are role-playing a same sex couple that has adopted, a bi-racial couple, or a single parent adoption? Perhaps there are some physical or mental health concerns in your background. **Please consult your instructor as you develop your character prior to the group exercise.**

Character: _____

_____

_____

_____

_____

_____

_____

_____

_____

_____

_____

_____

_____

You will also want to behave in a genuine manner while the group is in session. For instance, if you are unclear about something the facilitator(s) say, then you should express yourself honestly and seek clarity.

OBSERVER TASKS

Your role for this exercise is that of an **observer**. You have had or will have a chance to facilitate or participate in an exercise in your class, but during this group process experience you should sit quietly around the perimeter of the group. You will be assessing the performance of the group facilitators and at a later time will share your professional observations with other group exercise participants.

1) Use the following chart to help with your expectations and observations. Here are some questions to get you started: "What do you expect to take place during this group?" "What do you expect to see the facilitators doing?" "Which social work knowledge, values, and skills do you expect to be present in this adoptive family group meeting?" "Are there concepts of group practice that you think will be particularly helpful to the facilitators as they conduct their work?"

Expectations Before the Group Session	Observations During the Group Session
Knowledge:	Knowledge:
Skills:	Skills:
Values:	Values:
Other:	Other:

REFLECTING ON THE GROUP SESSION

A critical portion of this learning exercise is the processing that takes place immediately after the exercise. At the end of the group, all students will have the opportunity to participate in a post-group reflection exercise. The purpose of this reflection is to process the experiences of the group session and to understand the meaning of what transpired.

This process typically begins with the student group facilitators describing their experience leading the group. **Group facilitators**: you are expected to share the thoughts and emotions that you experienced during the group. Most importantly, you will provide a critique of your work that includes a **balanced assessment** of your strengths and areas for improvement. Then, each **participating group member**, including the joker(s), should use the "round robin" technique to provide balanced feedback for the facilitators. Lastly, the **observers** will comment on the exercise.

All members of the class (facilitators, group members, observers, and jokers) should consider the knowledge, skills and values that were demonstrated during the group exercise. In addition, feedback and reflection upon what was absent during the experience that perhaps could have assisted with group progress will make for meaningful group discussion. Our hope for you during this reflection exercise is that you are able to consider your own skills and the skills of your colleagues in context with what you've learned thus far in your curriculum and in this course in particular.

SUMMARY, KEY CONCEPTS, AND PRINCIPLES

You have just had the unique experience of participating in a post adoption family group. Hopefully this exercise was interesting and contributed to your understanding of the complexities of group work. As you take time to reflect on the session and the social work knowledge, skills, and values that were manifested in the experience, you might consider any one or more of the following key concepts and principles:

Ecological theory
Systems theory
Multicultural perspectives
Strengths perspectives
Feminist theory
Queer theory

Conflict theories
Cognitive development
Identity development
Attachment Theory
Adolescent Grief and Loss dynamics

WEB RESOURCES

Adopting.org
http://www.adopting.org
For those seeking to become adoptive parents. Information about who can adopt, the homestudy, procedures, terms, options, costs, agencies, facilitators, and professionals for domestic and international adoptions.

Adoption Resources
http://www.adoptionresources.org/about.html
The primary purpose of Adoption Resources is to serve the best interests of children, so that each child will be raised in a permanent and loving family. At Adoption Resources, we strive to provide services that protect the dignity of children, birth parents, adoptive families, and foster families. Our comprehensive serv-

ices provide all those involved in adoption with support and counseling, before, during, and after placement.

Adoption.com
http://about.adoption.com/
Adoption.com is committed to helping as many children as possible find loving, permanent homes. We also provide critical information at the decision-making moment to women facing crisis pregnancies. We assist adoptees and birthparents to find birth families, and we help hopeful adoptive parents make adoption dreams come true. We are especially committed to helping special needs children in the U.S. and around the world, who otherwise wouldn't be able to find families.

Child Welfare Information Gateway
http://www.childwelfare.gov/adoption/
Resources on all aspects of domestic and intercountry adoption, including adoption from foster care. Includes information for prospective and adoptive parents; information about searching for birth relatives; and resources for professionals on recruiting adoptive families, preparing children and youth, supporting birth parents, and providing postadoption services.

CHAPTER 10

A GROUP PRACTICE EXERCISE WITH

ADULTS WITH SUBSTANCE ABUSE DISORDERS

ERIN SIVIL, STEPHEN ERICH & HEATHER KANENBERG

By the end of this exercise, you should be able to demonstrate:

- Theoretical knowledge associated with group functioning.

- Evidence of competence related to the use of group work skills via the in-class group facilitation exercise.

- Theoretical knowledge, appropriate terminology, and issues related to individuals with substance abuse disorders (ex: treatment options, relapse prevention, issues with withdrawal, etc.).

- Theoretical knowledge and general issues related to the development of young adults and middle-aged individuals

BEFORE YOU BEGIN

The purpose of this role-playing exercise is to practice group leadership skills, to expose you to group dynamics, and diversity issues, and to provide information about substance abuse disorders among young and middle-aged adults. It will be important that you take time both in and out of class to prepare for such a task. It is expected that you will have been exposed to theory and information related to substance use, abuse, and treatment. Some background information to aid in your preparation: Prior to facilitating the group, participating students should have a pre-existing knowledge-base of group theories and skills. Students should also take the time to familiarize themselves with theories, issues, and terms related to human development and substance abuse. This includes, but is not limited to, dual diagnosis or comorbidity, addiction, detoxification, and relapse. The exercise should take no longer than a single class period once the students have studied and reviewed the necessary materials. The group should consist of approximately ten to fifteen members, including the group facilitators.

If you don't consider yourself familiar with this information or prepared for the exercise, you'll need to review some of this essential content in order to aid in your effectiveness. Feel free to use the web resources at the end of the exercise, the initial chapters of the book, the bibliography at the end of the text, your other textbooks, and also your instructor as resources to help you prepare.

GROUP EXERCISE:
ADULTS WITH SUBSTANCE ABUSE DISORDERS

You and your co-leader have been selected to facilitate a substance abuse support/educational group for a portion of the class. The exercise typically runs between 45-60 minutes.

SCENARIO

The purpose of the group is to provide a stable support system, to foster a healthy transition into a sober life-style by focusing on abstinence, and to improve interpersonal skills. Common issues generally experienced by this population include strain on family and peer relationships, mental and physical health concerns, withdrawal symptoms, homelessness, and social stigma.

This is a closed group that meets for one hour, three times a week for twelve weeks. Having met only twice before, all members are in the beginning phase of group work. During this phase of group-life, members are beginning to establish their own personal understanding of roles and norms. They are typically concerned with trust and safety in the group process and what is expected of them. Members in the initial stage of group work are still assessing their feelings and thoughts about you as the group leader(s), and other participating members. The group consists of mostly white, upper class, young and middle-aged adults. For today's meeting, you and your co-leader are planning to lead a discussion about relapse prevention. This can include information about recognizing warning signs (triggers) and how to construct a relapse prevention plan.

GROUP FACILITATOR TASKS

You and your co-leader are Hispanic social workers (LBSW's) facilitating a substance abuse group for young and middle aged adults.

1) To begin, you and your co-facilitator will want to conduct some research to develop your identity and some context for this role. *See the Character Profile assignment in Group Member Section.*

2) Prior to the group, you will need to develop an agenda for your session. Jot down some ideas of what you will need to include in your agenda. Feel free to use the following space to develop your agenda with your co-leader.   If you need some assistance, review the "Before you Begin" and "Scenario" portions of the exercise. You can also use the sample agendas in Appendix 1 as a guide. You will need to make the agenda available to your members in some way. You can post the agenda or distribute a copy of it to each participant on the day of the exercise (feel free to be creative with how this is done). Talk with your instructor about which is the best way to proceed.

_____

_____

_____

_____

_____

_____

_____

_____

_____

_____

_____

_____

_____

_____

_____

_____

You will want to keep in mind the following points while the group is in session:

- Motivating non-voluntary clients.
- Introduce group members, if necessary.
- Present your agenda to the members in some form, checking for agreement on the proposed items.
- Prepare, explain, and discuss the structure of the meeting.
- Use skills to foster understanding of the purpose and goals of the group.
- Use skills to facilitate task accomplishment within the group.
- Respond purposely to questions, comments, and concerns of members.
- Facilitate the group process-using available skill set.
- Develop and implement your plan for ending this group session.

ROLES FOR GROUP MEMBERS

Prior to the beginning of the group, you, with the assistance of your instructor, will get yourself "centered," if necessary, so that you may be able to engage in role playing as members of the adults with substance abuse disorders group that is concerned with providing psycho-educational tools to help prevent relapse.

1) In this exercise, there are several participants but no identified roles or character descriptions for them. **Before you start,** get together with the other members to identify your role and character. You will want to assume the identity and story of a member prior to the group exercise. To help you become more acquainted with your role, develop a **character profile** about the person you are playing, describing her/his character, her/his age and "story," how she/he came to be members, and her/his status in the group.

As you develop your character, we encourage you to ensure diversity is present in all its many forms within the group. As you consider who you will be and your concerns, consider whether or not you will represent an oppressed group. Will you role-play a member with physical limitations, a person that has been a victim of a crime, someone that has a non-traditional family structure, or a group member with hearing loss? **Please consult your instructor as you develop your character prior to the group exercise.**

Character: _____

_____

_____

_____

_____

_____

_____

_____

_____

_____

_____

_____

You will also want to function in a genuine manner while the group is in session. For instance, if you are unclear about something the facilitator(s) say, then you should express yourself honestly and seek clarity.

OBSERVER TASKS

Your role for this exercise is that of an **observer**. You have had or will have a chance to facilitate or participate in an exercise in your class, but during this group process experience you should sit quietly around the perimeter of the group. You will be assessing the performance of the group facilitators and at a later time will share your professional observations with other group exercise participants.

1) Use the following chart to help with your expectations and observations. Here are some questions to get you started: "What do you expect will happen during this group?" "What do you expect to see the facilitators doing?" "Which social work knowledge, values, and skills do you expect to be present in this psycho-educational group?" "Are there concepts of group practice that you think will be particularly helpful to the facilitators as they conduct their work?"

Expectations Before the Group Session	Observations During the Group Session
Knowledge:	Knowledge:
Skills:	Skills:
Values:	Values:
Other:	Other:

REFLECTING ON THE GROUP SESSION

A critical portion of this learning exercise is the processing that takes place immediately after the exercise. At the end of the group, all students will have the opportunity to participate in a post-group reflection exercise. The purpose of this reflection is to process the experiences of the group session and to understand the meaning of what transpired.

This process typically begins with the student group facilitators describing their experience leading the group. **Group facilitators**: you are expected to share the thoughts and emotions that you experienced during the group. Most importantly, you will provide a critique of your work that includes a **balanced assessment** of your strengths and areas for improvement. Then, each **participating group member**, including the joker(s), should use the "round robin" technique to provide balanced feedback for the facilitators. Lastly, the **observers** will comment on the exercise.

All members of the class (facilitators, group members, observers, and jokers) should consider the knowledge, skills and values that were demonstrated during the group exercise. In addition, feedback and reflection upon what was absent during the experience that perhaps could have assisted with group progress will make for meaningful group discussion. We hope

that during this reflection exercise you are able to consider your own skills and the skills of your colleagues in context with what you've learned thus far in your curriculum and in this course in particular.

SUMMARY, KEY CONCEPTS, AND PRINCIPLES

You have just had the unique experience of participating in a group for adults with substance abuse disorders. Hopefully this exercise was interesting and contributed to your understanding of the complexities of group work. As you take time to reflect on the session and the social work knowledge, skills, and values that were manifested in the experience, you might consider any one or more of the following key concepts and principles:

Person-in-Environment Perspective	Systems Theory
Strengths Perspective	Adlerian Theory
Ecological Theory	Empowerment Theory
Conflict Theory	Self-Determination
Social Learning Theory	Withdrawal & Relapse Prevention
Attachment Theory	

WEB RESOURCES

Join Together: Alcohol and Drug Policy, Prevention, and Treatment
www.jointogether.org
Join Together has merged into the National Center on Addiction and Substance Abuse (CASA*) at Columbia University, the only nationwide organization that brings together under one roof all the professional disciplines needed to study and combat abuse of all substances – alcohol, nicotine as well as illegal, prescription and performance enhancing drugs – in all sectors of society.

National Alcoholism Drug Addiction Information Center
www.addictioncareoptions.com/
If you are looking for help finding fast accurate answers and reliable information, call the alcoholism and drug addiction treatment hot line, anytime day or night for affordable addiction treatment options. Our services are always available and provided free of charge.

National Institute on Alcohol Abuse and Alcoholism
http://www.niaaa.nih.gov

To support and promote the best science on alcohol and health for the benefit of all by increasing the understanding of normal and abnormal biological functions and behavior relating to alcohol use, improving the diagnosis, prevention, and treatment of alcohol use disorders, and enhancing quality health care.

National Institute on Drug Abuse
http://www.nida.nih.gov
NIDA's mission is to lead the Nation in bringing the power of science to bear on drug abuse and addiction.

Office of National Drug Control Policy
http://www.whitehousedrugpolicy.gov
The goals of the program are to reduce illicit drug use, manufacturing, and trafficking, drug-related crime and violence, and drug-related health consequences.

Substance Abuse and Mental Health Services Administration
http://www.samhsa.gov
the Agency has sharply focused its mission on building resilience and facilitating recovery for people with or at risk for mental or substance use disorders.

CHAPTER 11

A GROUP PRACTICE EXERCISE WITH

DEMONSTRATING THE USE OF GROUP SUPERVISION

KAY SCHILLER

By the end of this exercise, you should be able to demonstrate:

- Evidence of theoretical knowledge regarding support and psycho-educational groups.
- Specific knowledge and skills related to the termination phase of group supervision.
- Identify essential components and nuances of group supervision.
- Competence related to the use of group work skills via the in-class group facilitation exercise.

BEFORE YOU BEGIN

The purpose of this exercise is to introduce students to practice issues and experiences in the termination phase of group supervision. It will be important that you take time both in and out of class to prepare for such a task.

Some background information to aid in your preparation: This group exercise assumes students will have been exposed to essential theoretical content including theory specifically related to group process, techniques, dynamics, supervisory issues and the ending stage of group development. Students will be expected to have working knowledge about the purpose and process of group supervision and how it relates to future practice as a social work professional. This exercise may be utilized in one or two class periods, or may even be utilized as an ongoing approach in a field seminar experience.

If you don't consider yourself familiar with this information or prepared for the exercise, you'll need to review some of this essential content in order to aid in your effectiveness. Feel free to use the web resources at the end of the exercise, the initial chapters of the book, the bibliography at the end of the text, your other textbooks, and also your instructor as resources to help you prepare.

GROUP EXERCISE:
DEMONSTRATING THE USE OF GROUP SUPERVISION

You and one of your peers are to facilitate a supervision group in the form of a social work supervision group for a portion of the class period (typically 45-60 minutes).

SCENARIO

You are a seasoned MSW social worker with five years of post MSW social work experience working in hospice settings. You are facilitating a social work supervision group for five BSW or MSW social workers. **The overall purpose of this social work supervision group** is to support the continued growth and development of the social work professional in their theoretical knowledge, skill, professional and ethical behavior, and cultural competence. Common issues include client case consultation, experience of transference and counter-transference, use of self, self-disclosure, organizational issues and conflicts, termination, honoring cultural diversity, and promoting the practice of professional self-care as covered in the NASW Code of Ethics.

It is understood by all students that the group has been meeting for three months and this is the closing meeting of the group. **This has been a closed group and was time-limited.** The social workers participating in this group are employed in hospice settings. **The purpose of this ending session** is to discuss termination with your fellow social workers, review the accomplishments of the group as a whole and as individual social workers, discuss professional growth and development of each colleague, and plan for the future.

GROUP FACILITATOR TASKS

You and one of your peers will be selected to facilitate a supervision group.

1) To begin, you and your co-facilitator will want to conduct some research to develop your identity and some context for this role. *See the Character Profile assignment in Group Member Section.*

2) Prior to the group, you will need to develop an agenda for your group meeting. Jot down some ideas of what you will need to include in your agenda. Feel free to use the following space to develop your agenda with your co-leader. If you need some assistance, review the "Before you Begin" and "Scenario" portions of the exercise. You can also use the sample agendas in Appendix 1 as a guide. You will need to make the agenda available to your members in some way. You can post the agenda or distribute a copy of it to each participant on the day of the exercise (feel free to be creative with how this is done). Talk with your instructor about which is the best way to proceed.

_____
_____
_____
_____
_____
_____
_____
_____
_____
_____
_____
_____
_____
_____
_____
_____
_____

You will want to keep in mind all or many of the following points while the group is in session:

- Create an environment conducive to healthy communication and understanding.
- Review group rules, procedures, and roles, if necessary.
- Respond purposely to questions, comments, and concerns of members.
- Facilitate the group process-using available skill set.
- Develop and implement your plan for ending this group supervision session and group.
- Refer to the chart on page 12 in Chapter 1 for more information about appropriate termination.

ROLES FOR GROUP MEMBERS

Prior to the beginning of the group, you, with the assistance of your instructor, will get yourself "centered," if necessary, so that you can engage in role playing as members of the group for demonstrating the use of group supervision.

1) In this exercise, there are several participants but no identified roles or character descriptions for them. **Before you start**, get together with the other members to identify your role and character. You will want to assume the identity and story of the member you choose prior to the group exercise. To help you become more acquainted with your role, develop a **character profile** about the person you are playing, describing her/his character, her/his age and "story,"' how she/he came to participate in the supervision group, and her/his current status in the group.

As you develop your character, we encourage you to ensure diversity is present in all its many forms within the group. As you consider who you will be and your concerns, consider whether or not you will represent an oppressed group. Perhaps you will role-play a professional with a hearing impairment or a physical limitation? Consider taking on the identity of a lesbian, gay, or transgendered social worker. **Please consult your instructor as you develop your character prior to the group exercise.**

Character: _____

_____

_____

_____

_____

_____

_____

_____

_____

_____

_____

_____

You will also want to function in a genuine manner while the group is in session. For instance, if you are unclear about something the facilitator(s) say, then you should express yourself honestly and seek clarity.

OBSERVER TASKS

Your role for this exercise is that of an **observer**. You have had or will have a chance to facilitate or participate in an exercise in your class, but during this group process experience you should sit quietly around the perimeter of the group. You will be assessing the performance of the group facilitators and at a later time will share your professional observations with other group exercise participants.

1) Use the following chart to help with your expectations and observations. Here are some questions to get you started:"What do you expect to see happen during this group?""What do you expect to see the facilitators doing?""Which social work knowledge, values, and skills do you expect to be present in this group for demonstrating the use of group supervision?" "Are there concepts of group practice that you think will be particularly helpful to the facilitators as they conduct their work?"

Expectations Before the Group Session	Observations During the Group Session
Knowledge:	Knowledge:
Skills:	Skills:
Values:	Values:
Other:	Other:

REFLECTING ON THE GROUP SESSION

A critical portion of this learning exercise is the processing that takes place immediately after the exercise. At the end of the group, all students will have the opportunity to participate in a post-group reflection exercise. The purpose of this reflection is to process the experiences of the group session and to understand the meaning of what transpired.

This process typically begins with the student group facilitators describing their experience leading the group. **Group facilitators**, you are expected to share the thoughts and emotions that you experienced during the group. Most importantly, you will provide a critique of your work that includes a **balanced assessment** of your strengths and areas for improvement. Then, each **participating group member**, including the joker(s), should use the "round robin" technique to provide balanced feedback for the facilitators. Lastly, the **observers** will comment on the exercise.

All members of the class (facilitators, group members, observers, and jokers) should consider the knowledge, skills and values that were demonstrated during the group exercise. In addition, feedback and reflection upon what was absent during the experience that perhaps could have assisted with group progress will make for meaningful group discussion. Our hope for you during this reflection exercise is that you are able to consider your own skills and the skills of your colleagues in context with what you've learned thus far in your curriculum and in this course in particular.

SUMMARY, KEY CONCEPTS, AND PRINCIPLES

You have just had the unique experience of participating in a task/support/psycho-educational group demonstrating skills in group supervision. Hopefully this exercise was interesting and contributed to your understanding of the complexities of group work. As you take time to reflect on the session and the social work knowledge, skills, and values that were manifested in the experience, you might consider any one or more of the following key concepts and principles:

Multicultural perspectives	Hospice Philosophy
Ecological Theory	Palliative Care
Systems Theory	Psychodynamic Theory
Empowerment Theory	Learning Theory
Strengths Perspectives	Social Exchange Theory
Conflict Theory	Field Theory
Feminist Theory	Supervision requirements: legal & ethical
Queer Theory	Grief and Loss

WEB RESOURCES

Texas Department of State Health Services
www.dshs.state.tx.us/socialwork
The Texas State Board of Social Worker Examiners (TSBSWE) regulates the profession of Social Work in Texas. The TSBSWE is a state agency with rule making authority governed by a nine member board appointed by the Governor, and is administratively attached to the Texas Department of State Health Services.

Clinical Supervision: A Practice Specialty of Clinical Social Work
www.abecsw.org/images/ABESUPERV2205ed406.pdf
This position statement is intended to be definitive and comprehensive in its treatment of Clinical Supervision as a specialty within the overall practice of Clinical Social Work.

Supervisor, Beware: Ethical Dangers in Supervision
www.socialworktoday.com/archive/julyaug2007p34.s html
Dewane, C. J. (2007). Supervisor, Beware: Ethical Dangers in Supervision. Social Work Today, 7(4). 34.

CHAPTER 12

A GROUP PRACTICE EXERCISE WITH

HOSPICE PLANNING FOR LOSS: CHILDREN WITH A PARENT WHO HAS A TERMINAL ILLNESS

MARY ANN NGUYEN, STEPHEN ERICH
& HEATHER KANENBERG

By the end of this exercise, you should be able to demonstrate:

- Evidence of theoretical knowledge of group functioning through your performance in the in-class group facilitation exercise.

- Evidence of theoretical knowledge of anticipatory grief and associated issues in children of terminally ill hospice patients through your performance in the group facilitation exercise.

- Evidence of competence related to the use of group work skills (ex: planning for termination, responding to challenging, selective attention, cueing and prompting, etc.).

- Evidence of multicultural competency.

BEFORE YOU BEGIN

The purpose of the exercise is to introduce students to group practice issues and experiences when working with children of the terminally ill. It will be important that you take time both in and out of class to prepare for such a task. It is expected that you will have been exposed to theory and information related to child development and grief and loss. Some background information to aid in your preparation: This exercise assumes that students will have been exposed to essential theoretical content including theory specifically related to family systems and anticipatory grief, bio-psychosocial and spiritual issues related to children, and the philosophy of hospice and palliative care. Students are expected to be familiar with the theories and skills relevant to the facilitation of therapeutic groups. This group experience is a one or two-class period process, depending on whether theoretical content is presented in a practice class setting or in previous class settings. Your instructor may modify this exercise in ways that best meet your needs.

If you don't consider yourself familiar with this information or prepared for the exercise, you'll need to review some of this essential content in order to aid in your effectiveness. Feel free to use the web resources at the end of the exercise, the initial chapters of the book, the bibliography at the end of the text, your other textbooks, and also your instructor as resources to help you prepare.

GROUP EXERCISE:
HOSPICE PLANNING FOR LOSS: CHILDREN WITH A PARENT WHO HAS A TERMINAL ILLNESS

You and one of your peers will co-facilitate a support/educational group for children of the terminally ill (typically 45 - 60 min). Student group facilitators will be given specific instructions they must follow before, during, and after the group.

SCENARIO

The purpose of the group is to provide emotional and psychological support, to reinforce healthy coping skills, to provide a perspective and understanding of the normal physical, behavioral, emotional, and spiritual reactions to anticipatory grief, and to prepare to say good-bye to the child's loved one.

Common issues include: the family feeling the effects of being in a long-term crisis mode; the healthy parent is consumed with care giving responsibilities; the children are unable to focus on school and other age appropriate activities; and the family experiences accumulated losses as the patient gradually declines.

It is understood by students that this is the third week of a four-week structured group, which is sponsored by CenterTown Hospice, and held in the family room of the inpatient unit. All group members are between the ages of 5 and 9 years. The topic of the third session is to learn techniques for self care, including progressive relaxation, positive self-talk, as well as the importance of getting adequate rest, exercise, and a balanced diet. Members will identify and discuss the people, places, activities, hobbies, music and literature which make them feel calm, comforted and relaxed. In addition, the topic of termination will need to be discussed and time should be allowed for closing comments from group members.

GROUP FACILITATOR TASKS

You and your co-leader are BSWs leading a support/educational group for children of terminally ill hospice patients. As student facilitators, you should possess a fundamental knowledge of group work and be familiar with the issues of death and dying as experienced by children.

1) To begin, you and your co-leader will want to conduct some research to develop your identity and some context for this role. *See the Character Profile assignment in Group Member section.*

2) As part of your session, there should be an exercise, in which members discuss what makes them feel calm, comforted and relaxed. Prepare this exercise and plan for when you'd like it to take place.

3) Prior to the group, you will need to develop an agenda (written or otherwise) for your members. Jot down some ideas of what you will need to include in your agenda. Feel free to use the following space to develop your agenda with your co-leader. If you need some assistance, review the "Before you Begin" and "Scenario" portions of the exercise. You can also use the sample agendas in Appendix 1 as a guide. You will need to make the agenda available to your members in some way. You can post the agenda or distribute a copy of it to each participant on the day of the exercise (feel free to be creative with how this is done). Talk with your instructor about which is best way to proceed.

_____

_____

_____

_____

_____

_____

_____

_____

_____

_____

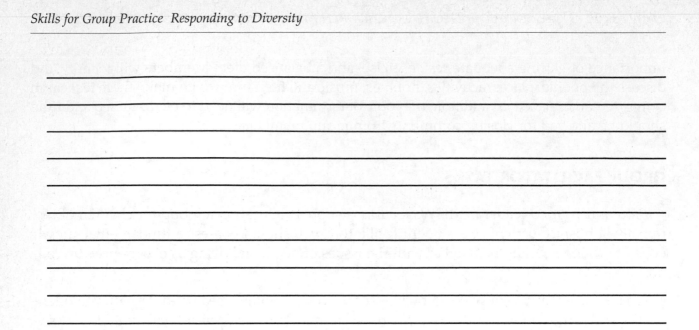

You will want to keep in mind any or all the following points while the group is in session:

- Create an environment conducive to healthy communication and understanding.
- Invite comments on the previous session and experiences of the past week.
- Present your agenda to the members in some form, checking for agreement on the proposed items.
- Prepare, explain, and discuss the structure of the meeting.
- Use skills to foster understanding of the purpose and goals of the group.
- Use skills to facilitate task accomplishment within the group.
- Respond purposely to questions, comments, and concerns of members.
- Facilitate the group process-using available skill set.
- Develop and implement your plan for ending this group session.
- Refer to the chart on page 12 in Chapter 1 for more information about appropriate termination.

ROLES FOR GROUP MEMBERS

Prior to the beginning of the group, as student group members, you will get yourself "centered" if necessary, so that you may be able to engage in role playing as members of the support group for children of the terminally ill.

1) **Before you start**, get together with the other members to identify your role and character. You will want to assume the identity and story of the member you choose prior to the group exercise. To help you become more acquainted with your role, develop a **character profile** about the person you are playing, describing the character, her/his age and "story," how she/he came to be a member, and her/his status in the group.

As you develop your character, we encourage you to ensure diversity is present in all its many forms within the group. As you consider who you will be and your concerns, consider whether or not you will represent an oppressed group. Perhaps you are a child from a same-sex parented household, or your parent is dying from complications related to

HIV/AIDS. Consider an identity where you are the child of a single parent or perhaps have previously been abused or neglected by your parent(s). **Please consult your instructor as you develop your character prior to the group exercise.**

Character: _____

_____

_____

_____

_____

_____

_____

_____

_____

_____

_____

_____

You will also want to behave in a genuine manner while the group is in session. For instance, if you are unclear about something the facilitator(s) say, then you should express yourself honestly and seek clarity.

OBSERVER TASKS

Your role for this exercise is that of an **observer**. You have had or will have a chance to facilitate or participate in an exercise in your class, but during this group process experience you should sit quietly around the perimeter of the group. You will be assessing the performance of the group facilitators and at a later time will share your professional observations with other group exercise participants.

1) Use the following chart to help with your expectations and observations. Here are some questions to get you started: "What do you expect to take place during this group?" "Which social work knowledge, values, and skills do you expect to be present in this planning for loss group?" "Are there concepts of group practice that you think will be particularly helpful to the facilitators as they conduct their work?"

Expectations Before the Group Session	Observations During the Group Session
Knowledge:	Knowledge:
Skills:	Skills:
Values:	Values:
Other:	Other:

REFLECTING ON THE GROUP SESSION

A critical portion of this learning exercise is the processing that takes place immediately after the exercise. At the end of the group, all students will have the opportunity to participate in a post-group reflection exercise. The purpose of this reflection is to process the experiences of the group session and to make meaning of what transpired.

This process typically begins with the student group facilitators describing their experience leading the group. **Group facilitators**: you are expected to share the thoughts and emotions that you experienced during the group. Most importantly, you will provide a critique of your work that includes a **balanced assessment** of your strengths and areas for improvement. Then, each **participating group member**, including the joker(s), should use the "round robin" technique to provide balanced feedback for the facilitators. Lastly, the **observers** will comment on the exercise.

All members of the class (facilitators, group members, observers, and jokers) should consider the knowledge, skills and values that were demonstrated during the group exercise. In addition, feedback and reflection upon what was absent during the experience that perhaps could have assisted with group progress will make for meaningful group discussion. We hope

that during this reflection exercise   you will be able to consider your own skills and the skills of your colleagues in context with what you've learned thus far in your curriculum and in this course in particular.

SUMMARY, KEY CONCEPTS, AND PRINCIPLES

You have just had the unique opportunity to participate in a planning for loss group with children. The experience was hopefully interesting and added to your understanding of the complexities of group work. As you take time to reflect on the group experience and the social work knowledge, skills, and values that were manifest in the experience, you might consider any one or more of the following key concepts and principles:

Systems Theory
Feminist Theory
Strengths Perspectives
Multicultural Perspectives
Conflict Theory

Group norms and roles
Death, Dying, Loss & Grief
Developmental theories relevant for children
NASW Statement on Palliative Care
Queer Theory
Buddhism

WEB RESOURCES

American Hospice Foundation
http://www.americanhospice.org/
American Hospice Foundation is proud to be a part of a collaborative effort of a large number of health care organizations to improve the quality and affordability of health care.

Association for Death Education and Counseling
http://www.adec.org/
ADEC is one of the oldest interdisciplinary organizations in the field of dying, death and bereavement. Its nearly 2,000 members include a wide array of mental and medical health personnel, educators, clergy, funeral directors and volunteers.

Bo's Place
http://www.bosplace.org/
Bo's Place is a bereavement center offering grief support services to children, ages 3 to 18, and their families who have experienced the death of a child or an adult in their immediate family, as well as programs for grieving adults. Bo's Place is founded on the belief that grieving children sharing their experiences with each other greatly helps in their grief journey.

National Hospice Work Group (NHWG)
http://www.nhwg.org/
A professional coalition of executives from some of the nation's largest and most innovative hospices, The National Hospice Work Group (NHWG) is committed to increasing access to hospice and palliative care. For more than 20 years members have made significant contributions to the care of patients facing life-threatening disease. As the century turns, we intend to advance even further, through advocacy, research and education, the proven model of care for people affected by profound disease.

Texas and New Mexico Hospice Organization
http://www.txnmhospice.org/Education.html
The Texas & New Mexico Hospice Organization, grounded in hospice philosophy and standards, advocates excellence in services, promotes ethical practices, and fosters education and research. It assists its membership network to provide care that enhances the quality of life for patients and their families experiencing a life-limiting illness.

CHAPTER 13

A GROUP PRACTICE EXERCISE WITH

COUPLES WHO HAVE ONE PARTNER WITH A TERMINAL FORM OF CANCER

STEPHEN ERICH & HEATHER KANENBERG

By the end of this exercise, you should be able to demonstrate:

- Evidence of theoretical knowledge of group functioning with couples.

- Evidence of theoretical knowledge of grief processes.

- Knowledge of terminology related to cancer, palliative care, and hospice philosophy.

- Knowledge of the various types of relationships between social workers and physicians and other hospital- based professionals and paraprofessionals.

- Evidence of competence related to the use of group work skills via the in-class group facilitation exercise, including couple work.

BEFORE YOU BEGIN

The purpose of this chapter is to introduce students to group practice issues and experiences when working with older couples in a hospital setting, one of which has a terminal form of cancer. It will be important that you take time both in and out of class to prepare for such a task. As background to aid in your preparation, this exercise assumes students will have been exposed to essential theoretical content, including theory specifically related to grief work, and issues related to cancer, palliative care, and hospice philosophy. Students are also expected to be familiar with language appropriate for working with this population, understanding the relationship between social workers and physicians, as well as theory and skills relevant to the facilitation of therapeutic groups. The exercise, as described here, is a one or two-class period process depending on whether theoretical content is presented in the current class or a previous one. Your instructor may modify this exercise in ways that best meet your needs.

If you don't consider yourself familiar with this information or prepared for the exercise, you'll need to review some of this essential content in order to aid in your effectiveness. Feel free to use the web resources at the end of the exercise, the initial chapters of the book, the bibliography at the end of the text, your other textbooks, and also your instructor as resources to help you prepare.

GROUP EXERCISE:
COUPLES WHO HAVE ONE PARTNER WITH A TERMINAL FORM OF CANCER

You and one of your peers will co-facilitate this support/educational group with an emphasis on facilitating couple communication regarding the eventual death of their partner. This exercise will typically last 45-60 minutes.

SCENARIO

Group membership consists of couples, each including at least one adult with cancer, who until recently, has also been undergoing aggressive treatment to combat the disease. Membership is predicated on the treating physician's recommendation that these patients now have less than 6 months to live. All members of this group are at least sixty years old. The purpose of the group is to facilitate each couple's understanding of the disease process, palliative care, and hospice philosophy, while also providing a milieu that supports members expressing issues related to grief and loss. Thus, this group is part psycho-educational and part supportive in nature. This is a time-limited, closed group (9 sessions). You are starting the 8th session. The group members are closely-knit and have shared much with one another. None of the group members have acknowledged that the last meeting of the group is two weeks away. Your task is to address the group membership's denial of the end of the group and introduce the process of termination with members, their partners, the group as a whole, and, for some members, with life on earth. This must be done. But it must be done with great care and sensitivity to each member of the group. As the leader(s), one or both of you may also be experiencing grief and loss. When introducing this subject, the leader should demonstrate awareness of the different manifestations of grief and loss and the different cultural variations in how grief and loss is understood and manifested. Be cautious of "imposing" your own values on this process. Be aware of the limitations of your competence.

GROUP FACILITATOR TASKS

You and your co-leader (BSWs) are facilitating a couples group at a metropolitan medical center. As student facilitators, you should possess a fundamental knowledge of group work and be familiar with the cultural backgrounds of participating couples.

1) To begin, you and your co-facilitator will want to conduct some research to develop your identity and some context for this role. *See the Character Profile assignment in Group Member Section.*

2) Prior to the group, you will need to develop an agenda for your members. Feel free to use the following space to develop your agenda with your co-leader. If you need some assistance, review the "Before you Begin" and "Scenario" portions of the exercise. You can also use the sample agendas in Appendix 1 as a guide. You will need to make the agenda available to your members in some way. You can post the agenda or distribute a copy of it to each participant on the day of the exercise (feel free to be creative with how this is done). Talk with your instructor about which is the best way to proceed.

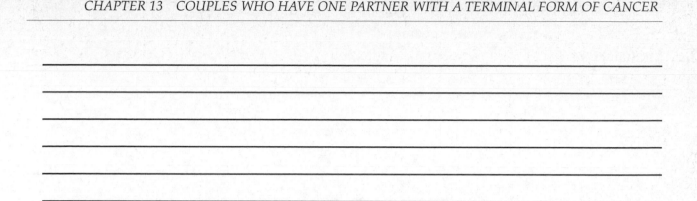

You will want to keep in mind the following points while the group is in session:

- Present your agenda to the members in some form, checking for agreement on the proposed items.
- Prepare, explain, and discuss the structure of the meeting.
- Use skills to foster understanding of the purpose and goals of the group.
- Use skills to facilitate task accomplishment within the group.
- Respond purposely to questions, comments, and concerns of members.
- Facilitate the group process-using available skill set.
- Develop and implement your plan for ending this group session.
- Refer to page the chart on page 12 in Chapter 1 for more information about appropriate termination.

ROLES FOR GROUP MEMBERS

Prior to the beginning of the group, you, with the assistance of your instructor, will get yourself "centered," if necessary, so that you will be able to engage in role playing as members of the Grief group for couples who have one partner with a terminal form of cancer that is concerned with psycho-education and support for the grieving members.

1) In this exercise, there are several participants but no identified roles or character descriptions for them. **Before you start**, get together with the other members to identify your role and character as well as that of your partner. You will want to assume the identity and story of the member you identify prior to the group exercise. To help you become more acquainted with your role, develop a **character profile** about the person you are playing, describing her/his character, her/his age and "story,"' how she/he came to the group, and her/his status in the group.

As you develop your character, we encourage you to ensure diversity is present in all its many forms within the group. As you consider who you will be and your concerns, consider whether or not you will represent an oppressed group. Are you in a relationship with a person of a different race or ethnicity? Are you a same-sex couple? Perhaps you practice a different faith or sense of spirituality. Or perhaps you or your partner are veterans? **Please consult your instructor as you develop your character prior to the group exercise.**

Character: _____

_____

_____

_____

_____

_____

_____

_____

_____

_____

_____

_____

You will also want to function in a genuine manner while the group is in session. For instance, if you are unclear about something the facilitator(s) say, then you should express yourself honestly and seek clarity.

OBSERVER TASKS

Your role for this exercise is that of an **observer**. You have had or will have a chance to facilitate or participate in an exercise in your class, but during this group process experience you should sit quietly around the perimeter of the group. You will be assessing the performance of the group facilitators and at a later time will share your professional observations with other group exercise participants.

1) Use the following chart to help with your expectations and observations. Here are some questions to get you started:"What do you expect to happen during this group?""What do you expect to see the facilitators doing?""Which social work knowledge, values, and skills do you expect to be present in this psycho-educational/support group?" "Are there concepts of group practice that you think will be particularly helpful to the facilitators as they conduct their work?"

Expectations Before the Group Session	Observations During the Group Session
Knowledge:	Knowledge:
Skills:	Skills:
Values:	Values:
Other:	Other:

REFLECTING ON THE GROUP SESSION

A critical portion of this learning exercise is the processing that takes place immediately after the exercise. At the end of the group, all students will have the opportunity to participate in a post-group reflection exercise. The purpose of this reflection is to process the experiences of the group session and to understand the meaning of what transpired.

This process typically begins with the student group facilitators describing their experience leading the group. **Group facilitators**: you are expected to share the thoughts and emotions that you experienced during the group. Most importantly, you will provide a critique of your work that includes a **balanced assessment** of your strengths and areas for improvement. Then, each **participating group member**, including the joker(s), should use the "round robin" technique to provide balanced feedback for the facilitators. Lastly, the **observers** will comment on the exercise.

All members of the class (facilitators, group members, observers, and jokers) should consider the knowledge, skills and values that were demonstrated during the group exercise. In addition, feedback and reflection upon what was absent during the experience that perhaps could have assisted with group progress will make for meaningful group discussion. We hope

that during this reflection exercise you are able to consider your own skills and the skills of your colleagues in context with what you've learned thus far in your curriculum and in this course in particular.

SUMMARY, KEY CONCEPTS, AND PRINCIPLES

You have just had the unique experience of participating in a Group for couples dealing with terminal illness. Hopefully this exercise was interesting and contributed to your understanding of the complexities of group work. As you take time to reflect on the session and the social work knowledge, skills, and values that were manifested in the experience, you might consider any one or more of the following key concepts and principles:

Multicultural Perspective	Queer Theory
Strengths Perspective	Grief/Loss Theories
Systems Theory	Group norms and roles
Ecological Theory	Empowerment
Conflict Theory	Cultural Diversity
Feminist Theory	Human development related to older persons (60+)

WEB RESOURCES

American Cancer Society
http://www.cancer.org/docroot/home/index.asp
General information on all aspects of cancer including facts, treatment, and support groups.

American Cancer Society
http://www.cancer.org/docroot/SPC/content/SPC_1_ Sexuality_and_Cancer.asp?sitearea=SPC&view-mode=print&
Sex and the couple facing cancer.

Cancer.Net
http://www.cancer.net/patient/Coping/Relationships+ and+Cancer/Family+Life
Cancer and family life. Dealing with grief and the importance of communication

The Jewish Bereavement Project
http://www.jewishbereavement.com/counselors.html
The Jewish Bereavement Project has been designed to provide information to help you, or someone you care for, find a way through the journey of mourning.

WebMD
http://www.webmd.com/cancer/news/20080306/can-cer-how-couples-handle-stress?src=RSS_PUBLIC
Cancer: How couples handle stress

CHAPTER 14

A GROUP PRACTICE EXERCISE WITH

ADULT PAROLEES

STEPHEN ERICH & HEATHER KANENBERG

By the end of this exercise, you should be able to demonstrate:

- Students will demonstrate knowledge of the mission and goals of the state's Mental Health, Department of Justice, and Commission on Alcohol and Drug Abuse Authority agencies.

- Students will demonstrate knowledge of the topics of assertiveness, aggressiveness, passiveness, and passive-aggressiveness.

- Students will demonstrate knowledge of the strengths and weaknesses associated with services designed for adult parolees (including recidivism rates and differential treatment by race and other factors).

- Students will demonstrate evidence of competence related to the use of group work (such as working with non-voluntary clients, coaching, modeling, etc.).

BEFORE YOU BEGIN

The purpose of the group is to facilitate group member's reintegration into their respective communities and to reduce recidivism rates. It will be important that you take time both in and out of class to prepare for such a task. It is expected that you will have been exposed to theory and information related to reintegration issues with adult parolees.   A bit of background to aid in your preparation: The group is sponsored through a collaborative effort between the Mental Health/Mental Retardation Authority (MHMRA), the Department of Criminal Justice (DCJ), and the Commission on Alcohol and Drug Abuse Authority (CADAA). Sponsorship for the group originates from a grant awarded by National Institute of Mental Health (NIMH). The parolee group represents one piece of a complex intervention strategy that was funded for three years. Group members are co-enrolled in each of these helping systems as needed. Representatives of each agency jointly develop "Master Treatment Plans". Treatment plan options may include specific services for issues related to chemical dependency and mental health issues if needed. One case-manager (funded through the NIMH grant) is assigned to facilitate achievement of the goals on the treatment plan. Examples of services include but are not limited to temporary living residences (halfway houses), GED courses, financial aid for college, job preparation and job coaching courses, medication, management services, and individual, family, and group treatment as needed. You are subject to the guidelines and rules set forth by your sponsoring agencies and the outcomes specified in the grant. Your participants generally have the following characteristics: poor education and job histories, poor social skills, poor coping strategies poor credit, problems with alcohol and substance abuse, strained or fragmented families systems, and unhealthy support systems.

If you don't consider yourself familiar with this information or prepared for the exercise, you'll need to review some of this essential content in order to aid in your effectiveness. Feel free to use the web resources at the end of the exercise, the initial chapters of the book, the bibliography at the end of the text, your other textbooks, and also your instructor as resources to help you prepare.

GROUP EXERCISE:
ADULT PAROLEES

You and your co-leader are facilitating a group for adult parolees recently released from prison (typically 45 minutes – 1 hour).

SCENARIO

The group of parolees is meeting for the fourth time of this ten session group. Meetings occur once a week. Each meeting is scheduled to last 45 minutes to 1 hour. Parolees are required to attend these meetings. You are required to provide evidence that members are in fact attending all of these meetings (co-facilitators decide how to do this). As facilitators, you will employ a variety of tools/processes in your attempt to achieve stated goals. These include some didactic presentations with opportunities for group discussion (e.g., problem solving strategies); mutual support; role playing; coaching; and modeling. Today, you and your co-leader have decided to have members engage in role-plays. The role-play is designed to help members practice and refine problem-solving skills. The specific focus is "how to behave assertively" (not passive, passive aggressive, or aggressively). To do this, you must introduce the subject and provide some definitions and examples of assertive behavior as well as the less desirable forms of relating. Then ask for two volunteers for a role-play. One person will be practicing his new skills (assertiveness). The other person is a volunteer in the role-play who you instruct to play a role like a boss, co-worker, spouse or friend - preferably, someone important to the member who is practicing the new skill. Your job is to introduce the topic, model the expected behavior, facilitate the role-play, and have the group transition into a discussion about the topic. Remember these group members are required to attend your group. Their motivation varies from simple or reluctant compliance to the rules, to really trying to change their behavior. Several group members have a significant history of aggressive behavior. Their social skills, in general, are quite limited at this time.

GROUP FACILITATOR TASKS

You and your co-leader are facilitating a group for adult parolees recently released from prison.

1) To begin, you and your co-facilitator will want to conduct some research to develop your identity and some context for this role. *See the Character Profile assignment in Group Member Section.*

2) Prior to the group, you will need to develop an agenda for your group meeting. Feel free to use the following space to develop your agenda with your co-leader.   If you need some assistance, review the "Before you Begin" and "Scenario" portions of the exercise. You can also use the sample agendas in Appendix 1 as a guide. You will need to make the agenda available to your members in some way. You can post the agenda or distribute a copy of it to each participant on the day of the exercise (feel free to be creative with how this is done). Talk with your instructor about which is the best way to proceed.

_____

_____

_____

_____

_____

_____

_____

_____

_____

_____

_____

_____

_____

_____

_____

_____

_____

_____

You will want to keep in mind the following points while the group is in session:

- Motivating non-voluntary clients.
- Present your written agenda to the members in some form, checking for consent on the proposed items.
- Prepare, explain, and discuss the structure of the meeting.
- Use skills to foster understanding of the purpose and goals of the group if necessary.
- Respond purposely to questions, comments, and concerns of members.
- Facilitate the group process-using available skill set.
- Develop and implement your plan for ending this group session.

ROLES FOR GROUP MEMBERS

Prior to the beginning of the group, you, with the assistance of your instructor, will get yourself "centered" if necessary, so that you will be able to engage in role playing as members of the Adult Parolee Group that is concerned with attempting to aid in reintegration.

1) In this exercise, there are several participants but no identified roles or character descriptions for them. **Before you start**, get together with the other members to identify your role and character. Keep in mind members have various levels of motivation to participate in this group. You will want to be sure that you have persons role-playing across this spectrum. You will want to assume the identity and story of the member you choose prior to the group exercise. To help you become more acquainted with your role, develop a **character profile** about the person you are playing, describing her/his character, her/his age, the "story" of how she/he came to the parolee group, and her/his status in the group.

As you develop your character, we encourage you to ensure diversity is present in all its many forms within the group. As you consider who you will be and your concerns, consider whether or not you will represent an oppressed group. Will you be someone that is particular-ly vulnerable as an adult parolee because of race, ethnicity, type of conviction, physical ability, age, sexual orientation/gender identity, etc.? **Please consult your instructor as you develop your character prior to the group exercise.**

Character: _____

_____

_____

_____

_____

_____

_____

_____

_____

_____

_____

_____

You will also want to function in a genuine manner while the group is in session. For instance, if you are unclear about something the facilitator(s) say, then you should express yourself honestly and seek clarity.

OBSERVER TASKS

Your role for this exercise is that of an **observer**. You have had or will have a chance to facil-itate or participate in an exercise in your class, but during this group process experience you should sit quietly around the perimeter of the group. You will be assessing the performance of the group facilitators and at a later time will share your professional observations with other group exercise participants.

1) Use the following chart to help with your expectations and observations. Here are some questions to get you started: "What do you expect will happen during this group?" "What do you expect to see the facilitators doing?" "Which social work knowledge, values, and skills do you expect to be present in this parolee group meeting?" "Are there concepts of group practice that you think will be particularly helpful to the facilitators as they conduct their work?"

Expectations Before the Group Session	Observations During the Group Session
Knowledge:	Knowledge:
Skills:	Skills:
Values:	Values:
Other:	Other:

REFLECTING ON THE GROUP SESSION

A critical portion of this learning exercise is the processing that takes place immediately after the exercise. At the end of the group, all students will have the opportunity to participate in a post-group reflection exercise. The purpose of this reflection is to process the experiences of the group session and to understand the meaning of what transpired.

This process typically begins with the student group facilitators describing their experience leading the group. **Group facilitators**: you are expected to share the thoughts and emotions that you experienced during the group. Most importantly, you will provide a critique of your work that includes a **balanced assessment** of your strengths and areas for improvement. Then, each **participating group member**, including the joker(s), should use the "round robin" technique to provide balanced feedback for the facilitators. Lastly, the **observers** will comment on the exercise.

All members of the class (facilitators, group members, observers, and jokers) should consider the knowledge, skills and values that were demonstrated during the group exercise. In addition, feedback and reflection upon what was absent during the experience that perhaps could have assisted with group progress will make for meaningful group discussion. Our hope for you during this reflection exercise is that you are able to consider your own skills and the skills of your colleagues in context with what you've learned thus far in your curriculum and in this course in particular.

SUMMARY, KEY CONCEPTS, AND PRINCIPLES

You have just had the unique experience of participating in a group for adult parolees working on reintegration. Hopefully this exercise was interesting and contributed to your understanding of the complexities of group work. As you take time to reflect on the session and the social work knowledge, skills, and values that were manifested in the experience, you might consider any one or more of the following key concepts and principles:

Systems Theory

Multicultural Perspective

Strengths Perspective

Ecological Theory

Feminist Theory

Queer Theory

Conflict Theory

Group norms and roles

Structure

Cohesion

Cultural Diversity

Teaching Skills

Role Modeling

Role Playing

Characteristics of assertiveness, passivity, passive aggressive, and aggression

WEB RESOURCES

National Institute of Mental Health

http://www.nimh.nih.gov/.

The mission of NIMH is to transform the understanding and treatment of mental illnesses through basic and clinical research, paving the way for prevention, recovery and cure.

Mental Health, Mental Retardation Authority-Harris County

http://www.mhmraharris.org/.

It shall be the mission of the Mental Health and Mental Retardation Authority of Harris County (MHMRA), within the resources available, to provide or ensure the provision of services and supports in a respectful fashion that are high quality, efficient, and cost effective such that persons with mental disabilities may live with dignity as fully functioning, participating, and contributing members of our community as possible, regardless of their ability to pay or third party coverage.

Texas Department of Criminal Justice.

http://www.tdcj.state.tx.us

National Institute of Chemical Dependency

http://www.nicd.us/halfwayhouselistingsnicd-magazine.html

National listings for Halfway houses.

Office of Juvenile Justice and Delinquency Prevention

http://ojjdp.ncjrs.org/

OJJDP, a component of the Office of Justice Programs, U.S. Department of Justice, accomplishes its mission by supporting states, local communities, and tribal jurisdictions in their efforts to develop and implement effective programs for juveniles. The Office strives to strengthen the juvenile justice system's efforts to protect public safety, hold offenders accountable, and provide services that address the needs of youth and their families.

United States Department of Justice

http://www.usdoj.gov

To enforce the law and defend the interests of the United States according to the law; to ensure public safety against threats foreign and domestic; to provide federal leadership in preventing and controlling crime; to seek just punishment for those guilty of unlawful behavior; and to ensure fair and impartial administration of justice for all Americans.

SECTION 4

TASK GROUPS

CHAPTER 15

A TASK-GROUP PRACTICE EXERCISE WITH

A SOCIAL ACTION COMMITTEE ADDRESSING NEIGHBORHOOD GANG VIOLENCE

NICOLE WILLIS

By the end of this exercise, you should be able to demonstrate:

- Skills in facilitating an interdisciplinary team.

- The use of research and data collection to inform assessment.

- An understanding of the relationship between poverty, oppression, and violence.

- The application of cultural competence as a part of the framework for building a community action team and community intervention plan.

- How social justice theories (social stratification, ethnocentrism, social construction, distributive justice, etc.) and systems theory apply to addressing neighborhood gang violence.

- An understanding of how the success of the community action team intervention can be measured/evaluated.

- Knowledge of gang culture.

- The capacity to identify your own cultural biases.

BEFORE YOU BEGIN

We recognize that the issues of gang violence and social action groups may or may not be areas that you are intimately familiar with. Therefore, it's probably best to take some time to consider the intricacies of the exercise. The purpose of this exercise is to expose social work students to task group practice issues when working with a social action team to address gang violence in a neighborhood. It is assumed that you will already be familiar with the concepts of cultural competency/diversity, oppression, social justice theories, macro-practice, inter-disciplinary practice, and evidence-based practice. If you are not familiar with these constructs, we suggest you take time in class or prior to engaging in this exercise to brush up on them. Perhaps consult the chapters at the beginning of this workbook, the web-resources at the end of this exercise, the bibliography at the end of the book, your other textbooks, your lecture notes, or have a discussion with faculty in your program to help you develop a reasonable level of comfort with your understanding of the material needed for the exercise.

Frequently, in neighborhoods with high levels of gang violence, various departments (i.e., the police department, the Mayor's office, the Anti-Gang Office, etc.) or agencies (i.e., local schools, Guardian Angels, religious entities) attempt to address gang violence as *individual* entities. However, these attempts have often achieved short-lived results. Your job as a social worker is to lead a community action team whose collaborative and multi-systemic approaches can help to effectively reduce gang violence in a manner that results in sustainable change.

If you don't consider yourself familiar with this information or prepared for the exercise, you'll need to review some of this essential content in order to aid in your effectiveness. Feel free to use the web resources at the end of the exercise, the initial chapters of the book, the bibliography at the end of the text, your other textbooks, and also your instructor as resources to help you prepare.

GROUP EXERCISE:
A SOCIAL ACTION COMMITTEE ADDRESSING
NEIGHBORHOOD GANG VIOLENCE

You and the Gang Interventionist are co-facilitators of this first committee meeting (typically 45-60 minutes).

SCENARIO

You are a third-year social worker at Marx High School. This school is located in a zip code that is 80% Hispanic, has a high poverty rate, and the second highest juvenile crime rate in the state. The high school received a 2-year grant to employ a Gang Interventionist to work one-on-one counseling students to help them get out of gangs (the most prominent gangs being the MS-13 and Southwest Cholos). However, this has not created much change in the amount of neighborhood gang violence. The number of gang-related shootings has increased significantly over the last few years. In fact, 3 students at your high school have been shot this year alone (one of which was fatal). During a meeting with the Gang Interventionist, you decide to work together to create a social action committee (7 people) to address the gang violence.

GROUP FACILITATOR TASKS

Your role is to co-facilitate a discussion with the committee members to explore what type of collaborative social action plan might be an effective way to reduce the gang violence in your zip code. You both decide to integrate two group models as a framework for facilitating the social action committee: (1) stages of group development, and (2) Graham and Barter (1999) phases of collaboration model. This will be the first of several meetings the social action committee will hold prior to the implementation of community action. Therefore, as co-facilitators you will demonstrate your skills by focusing on introductions, orienting members, discussing purpose of the committee, establishing confidentiality, ground rules and group structure, problem definition, discussion of gang violence issues, possible goals and objectives for the committee, individual tasks to be completed for the next meeting, as well as facilitate closure for the first meeting. In addition, you must assign someone to take the minutes for the meeting.

1) You and your co-leader the gang interventionist need to decide which 7 people and the organizations they represent that will be invited to participate on the social action committee. Describe the rationale for inviting the people you chose.

1. _Schools_ (social worker)
2. _Mental Health_ (Home based service)
3. _School - Police_   School Resource Officer
4. _CSU_   Dept.
5. _Mentoring program representative_
6. _Education Prevention Intervention_ — Gang Prevention program
7. _Community activist_ (Casa Churilagua) Community loggius
   Parents . or a parent

*You and your co-leader will need to share these with your instructor and your peers; this will help them to develop their character and prepare to participate fully in the group meeting.

2) Decide on logistics of the first team meeting in terms of location, time and duration of meeting. Explain your decision-making process.

City Hall

_____

_____

3) Prior to the group, you and your co-leader will need to develop an agenda for your group meeting. Feel free to use the following space to develop your agenda with your co-leader. If you need some assistance, review the "Before you Begin" and "Scenario" portions of the exercise. You can also use the sample agendas in Appendix 2 as a guide. You will need to make the agenda available to your members in some way. You can post the agenda or distribute a copy of it to each participant on the day of the exercise (feel free to be creative with how this is done). Talk with your instructor about how best to proceed.

_____

_____

_____

_____

_____

_____

_____

_____

_____

_____

_____

_____

_____

_____

You will want to keep in mind all or many of the following points while the group is in session:

- You are working to create an environment conducive to healthy communication and understanding.
- You'll need to facilitate introductions of group members.
- How will you prepare, explain, and discuss the structure of the meeting including the decision-making process that will be used.
- Use skills to foster understanding of the purpose and goals of the group.
- Use skills to facilitate task accomplishment within the group.

- Respond purposely to questions, comments, and concerns of members.
- Facilitate the group process-using your available skill set.
- Develop and implement your plan for ending this group session.

ROLES FOR GROUP MEMBERS

Prior to the beginning of the group exercise, you, with assistance of your instructor, will get yourself "centered," if necessary, so that both of you may be able to engage in role playing as members of the group that is concerned with reducing gang violence.

1) In this exercise, there are several participants with identified roles/characters. **Before you start,** get together with the other members to prepare for the exercise. Your two co-facilitators have developed a list of specific professionals from the community that are in attendance at the meeting. You will want to be sure that you are taking on one of these identities and you'll want to do it before the group exercise begins. To help you become more acquainted with your role, develop a **character profile** about the person you are playing, describing the character, their age and 'story', how they come to be in the role they are in and agency they work for, and their thoughts about the group.

As you develop your character, we encourage you to ensure diversity is present in all its many forms within the group. As you consider who you will be and your concerns, consider whether or not you will represent an oppressed group. Are you a former gang member? Are you a professional that has experienced violence and trauma or perhaps loss due to the issues in your community? Perhaps you'll role play a low-income parent of a child in a gang that also happens to be a professional invited to the meeting? **Please consult your instructor as you develop your character prior to the group exercise.**

Character: _____

_____

_____

_____

_____

_____

_____

_____

_____

_____

_____

_____

You will also want to function in a genuine manner while the group is in session. For instance, if you are unclear about something the facilitator(s) say, then you should express yourself honestly and seek clarity.

OBSERVER TASKS

Your role for this exercise is that of an **observer**. You have had or will have a chance to facilitate or participate in an exercise in your class, but during this group process experience you should sit quietly around the perimeter of the group. You will be assessing the performance of the group facilitators and at a later time will share your professional observations with other group exercise participants.

1) Use the following chart to help with your expectations and observations. Here are some questions to get you started: "What do you expect will happen during this group?""What do you expect to see the facilitators doing?""Which social work knowledge, values, and skills do you expect to be present in this social action committee on neighborhood gang violence?" "Are there concepts of group practice that you think will be particularly helpful to the facilitators as they conduct their work?"

Expectations Before the Group Session	Observations During the Group Session
Knowledge:	Knowledge:
Skills:	Skills:
Values:	Values:
Other:	Other:

REFLECTING ON THE GROUP SESSION

A critical portion of this learning exercise is the processing that takes place immediately after the exercise. At the end of the group, all students will have the opportunity to participate in a post-group reflection exercise. The purpose of this reflection is to process the experiences of the group session and to understand the meaning of what transpired.

This process typically begins with the student group facilitators describing their experience leading the group. **Group facilitators**: you are expected to share the thoughts and emotions that you experienced during the group. Most importantly, you will provide a critique of your work that includes a **balanced assessment** of your strengths and areas for improvement. Then, each **participating group member**, including the joker(s), should use the "round robin" technique to provide balanced feedback for the facilitators. Lastly, the **observers** will comment on the exercise.

All members of the class (facilitators, group members, observers, and jokers) should consider the knowledge, skills and values that were demonstrated during the group exercise. In addition, feedback and reflection upon what was absent during the experience that perhaps could have assisted with group progress will make for meaningful group discussion. Our hope for you during this reflection exercise is that you are able to consider your own skills and the skills of your colleagues in context with what you've learned thus far in your curriculum and in this course in particular.

SUMMARY, KEY CONCEPTS, AND PRINCIPLES

You have just experienced an initial meeting of a task group that is focused on reducing gang violence in your community. Hopefully this exercise was interesting and contributed to your understanding of the complexities of group work. As you take time to reflect on the session and the social work knowledge, skills, and values that were manifested in the experience, you might consider any one or more of the following key concepts and principles:

NASW Code of Ethics
Group Roles and Norms
Phases of Collaboration
Power within the Group
Systems theory
Multi-cultural perspective
Strengths perspective
Feminist theory
Empowerment theory
Conflict theory

Social justice theories: Distributive
    justice, social stratification, etc.
Human Development
Diversity Perspectives
Symbolic interaction theory
Labeling theory,
Transpersonal theories
Group Dynamics Theories
Social learning theory
Social capital theory

WEB RESOURCES

Harris County Protective Services for Children and Adults
http://www.hc-ps.org/whats_new.htm
This Harris County Protective Services for Children and Adults website includes a resource Directory for Harris County that lists a variety of non-profit agencies in the Houston area that provide specific services for children and adults. This is helpful not only in linking clients with specific resources, but also finding agencies who may be interested in collaborative teams for community change. Students can often expect to find similar web resources in their local/regional area.

National Criminal Justice Reference Serive
http://www.ncjrs.gov/spotlight/gangs/Summary.html
The U.S. Department of Justice Office of Justice Programs created this website, which includes detailed information on gangs, including statistics, funding resources, relevant policies, prevention/intervention programs, as well as informative publications.

Search Institute
http://www.search-institute.org/
The Search Institute provides information on the 40 internal and external developmental assets in youth that increase the likelihood of healthy transition from childhood to adulthood.

City of Houston – Anti-Gang Office
http://www.houstontx.gov/publicsafety/antigang/index.html
The Mayor's Anti-Gang office in Houston offers information about gang involvement, programs and services as well as speaker's bureau to educate staff, parents and the community about gang activity/involvement. Students can often expect to find similar web resources in their local/regional area.

The Campbell Collaboration
http://www.campbellcollaboration.org/
The Crime and Justice Coordinating Group (part of the Campbell Collaboration) is composed of researchers around the world whom review and critique studies published on the issue of delinquency and crime reduction. These researchers offer a variety of evidence-based, systematic reviews of studies testing the effectiveness of common intervention and prevention methods, such as boot camps and juvenile prevention programs. These researchers make conclusions about the overall effectiveness of prevention/intervention programs that readers at all levels of research knowledge can understand.

CHAPTER 16

A TASK GROUP PRACTICE EXERCISE WITH

A SOCIAL WORK POLITICAL ACTION COMMITTEE

AMY RUSSELL

By the end of this exercise, you should be able to demonstrate:

- Theoretical knowledge of task group functioning.

- Theoretical knowledge of the political process and advocacy in social work.

- Knowledge of Parliamentary Procedure and Roberts Rules of Order.

- Understanding of the National Association of Social Work Code of Ethics and ethical principles associated with working within political action committes.

- Competence with group work skills in a political arena.

BEFORE YOU BEGIN

Let's get centered and prepare for the exercise. The purpose of this particular exercise is to introduce you to the many different group practice issues and experiences that can surface when working as a social work political action committee (PAC) member. It will be important that you take time both in and out of class to prepare for such a task.

As a bit of background to aid in your preparation: This activity assumes that you have had a chance to study and develop an understanding of theoretical content that's important for task groups. This includes material on the task group process, Roberts Rules of Order, conflict theories, electoral politics, lobbying and activism, social work advocacy, social work ethics, fundraising and campaigning, and the political process. This is a lot of material, so if you're not clear about any portion of this, we recommend you take time now to review your notes, the web-resources at the end of this exercise, the bibliography at the end of the book, and/or other textbooks to refresh yourself. You might have to start this process the week prior to when this group exercise will actually take place in your classroom or lab. This exercise is based on the National Association of Social Workers Political Action for Candidate Election (PACE) trustee committees that exist across the country. The purpose of these social work groups, or PACs, is to enhance government relations, mobilize the vote, and to research and assess those candidates in elections that support social work values and to fundraise for candidates that share social work values. This group is bipartisan.

GROUP EXERCISE:
A SOCIAL WORK POLICTICAL ACTION COMMITTEE

Two students will be selected to facilitate the PAC Meeting for a portion of the class period (approximately 45-60 minutes). There is a third articulated role for a committee member that has some additional responsibilities of facilitation in this exercise – the staff lobbyist.

SCENARIO

This is a task group designed to meet client, organizational, and community needs during the legislative session. The group is open only for admission for new trustees at the beginning of the year when former trustees complete their tenure on the PAC; therefore, the group consists of both old timers and newcomers. The task group is open-ended. It is a formed group with a specific purpose focused on political and electoral government relations. The members interact at concentrated periods of time annually: a teleconference monthly for one hour, a summer conference to determine endorsements and organizational needs, and finally members facilitate PACE informational sessions and advocacy and lobbying educational trainings at the profession's annual conference. Work within the group is seasonal, depending on elections and legislative sessions. The members are approved on a competitive basis by administrators within the state professional organization and represent geographic regions throughout the state. Committee trustees serve three year terms and can only serve two consecutive terms, unless appointed to a leadership position. The PAC focuses solely on state government and elections.

You are operating in a mostly conservative(as opposed to liberal) state,   in which the Republican platform does not fit so well with social work values. (Conservatism is defined as a sociopolitical orientation focusing on traditional values and reduced governmental funding. Liberalism is defined as a sociopolitical orientation that focuses on increasing opportunity for all citizens through governmental spending. [Barker, 2003]).

The committee is experiencing its busiest time of the state biennium, as elections are approaching. At a meeting in July in the conservative state to review and determine endorsements based on geography, a conflict arises around the idea of endorsing Republicans who have legislative access to social work related committees (serving as committee members, chairpersons, etc). While the PAC is bipartisan, some republican platform stances conflict with social work values; however, the geographic district is republican controlled and the representative is chair of a human services committee, which social work must access during the legislative session. This access is gained through the PAC's endorsement.

GROUP FACILITATOR ROLES AND TASKS

You and your co-leader are the chair and vice chair of a state social work PAC. The chair and vice chair co- facilitate the meeting, but the Staff Lobbyist has an active role in the group. The purpose of this meeting is to determine the most effective candidate endorsements for the upcoming state general election. Nonpartisan endorsements include monetary contributions, endorsement letters, and mobilization of social workers for campaign volunteerism.

The chair is more conservative and the vice chair is more liberal, and the staff lobbyist needs specific endorsements to gain access to legislators appointed to social work relevant committees, such as Human Services, Public and Higher Education, Juvenile Justice and Family Issues, and Public Health Committees. This is further complicated as access to committees and politicians is necessary with the upcoming and critical legislative session. Remember: access is gained through support, which also entails monetary donations.

Specific group facilitator roles:

The roles for each of the facilitators are different, although their goal is the same, to reach consensus about candidate endorsements.

1. Chair of the PAC:

You are conservative, meaning you understand and are aware of social work values; however, you fall along the smaller government, moral "family" values lines of debate. You express that you embrace social work values and are aware of the conflicts in the political process and you verbally acknowledge this. You do, however, press the non-partisan stance of the PAC and remind trustees of the conservative state politics in which the PAC navigates. You facilitate and lead the entire PAC, but are having conflicts with other trustees over conservative values versus political endorsements.

2. Vice Chair of the PAC:

   You are more liberal than the chair, but you too acknowledge the necessity of non-partisan endorsements. You are aware of the conflicts between the chair and trustees. You are essentially a default mediator in this process. Assisting the chair, staff lobbyist, and trustees in the endorsement process is your main task.

Specific group facilitator tasks:

1. As you prepare, you and your co-leader should consider your roles and do research to help you become centered in your new identity. You may use the *Character Profile assignment* in the Group Member section to take notes. You should think thoroughly about your role play position prior to facilitating the group.

2. In this exercise, there is a clear goal for this PAC meeting. You and your co-chair should work to determine how the workload will be divided. Feel free to jot down your notes in the space provided (remember to refer to the sample Task Group Agenda in Appendix 2 if you need some help).

_____

_____

_____

_____

_____

_____

_____

_____

_____

_____

_____

_____

_____

_____

_____

_____

_____

_____

You will want to keep in mind any or all of the following points while the group is in session:

- Remember the task group process and the steps for resolving conflict.
- Name the process and conflicts.
- Ensure safety and limits of confidentiality are established.
- Facilitate consensual decision making if possible and adherence to Roberts Rules of Order.
- Ensure closure regarding in decisions and endorsements.
- Administer the stages of decision making in task groups.
- Maintain the non-partisan process of the PAC.
- Maintain the integrity and precedence of social work values.
- Ensure all voices are heard in the endorsement process.

ROLES FOR GROUP MEMBERS

You and the remaining trustees of the group have done your research and are ready to make your recommendations and put said recommendations to a committee vote. Some of these endorsements are conservative and some liberal. But you, as the committee are not interested in debating any conflict for the sake of argument. Further, you wish to get through the extensive list quickly and move on to planning for future mobilization and public awareness strategies in the limited time you have together.

1. In order for the PAC selection meeting to be successful, each member of the group representing trustees from around the state will need to determine the candidates of their choosing prior to entering the group exercise. Consult with your instructor to determine if she/he would like you to use the sample Voters Guide in APPENDIX 3 of this book, or if she/he has another option for you.

    Prior to the beginning of the group, you, with the assistance of your instructor, should get yourselves "centered" if necessary. This will facilitate your engagement in role playing as members of the PAC.

2. In this exercise, there are several participants but only a few identified roles and character descriptions for them. **Before you start**, get together with the other members to identify your role and character. You will want to assume the identity and story of the member you choose prior to the group exercise. To help you become more acquainted with your role, develop a **character profile** about the person you are playing, describing her/his character, her/his position on the issues, how she/he came to be a trustee, and her/his status in the group.

    As you develop your character, we'd like to encourage you to ensure diversity is present in all its many forms within the group. As you consider who you will be and your concerns, consider whether or not you will represent an oppressed group. Perhaps your positions are based on constituent/client needs that are particularly disenfranchised. You may choose to role-play a person of color or trustee with serious convictions around religion and this influences your decisions. Or perhaps you are an immigrant and working to advocate for immigrant rights. **Please consult your instructor as you develop your character prior to the group exercise.**

Character: _____

_____

_____

_____

_____

_____

_____

_____

_____

_____

_____

_____

_____

_____

You will also want to function in a genuine manner while the group is in session. For instance, if a group member is unclear about something your co-facilitators say, then you should express yourself honestly and seek clarity.

OBSERVER TASKS

Your role for this exercise is that of an **observer**. You have had or will have a chance to facilitate or participate in an exercise in your class, but during this group process experience you should sit quietly around the perimeter of the group. You will be assessing the performance of the group facilitators and at a later time will share your professional observations with other group exercise participants.

1) Use the following chart to help with your expectations and observations. Here are some questions to get you started: "What do you expect will happen during this group?""What do you expect to see the facilitators doing?""Which social work knowledge, values, and skills do you expect to be present in this PAC meeting?""Are there concepts of group practice that you think will be particularly helpful to the facilitators as they conduct their work?"

Expectations Before the Group Session	Observations During the Group Session
Knowledge:	Knowledge:
Skills:	Skills:
Values:	Values:
Other:	Other:

REFLECTING ON THE GROUP SESSION

A critical portion of this learning exercise is the processing that takes place immediately after the exercise. At the end of the group, all students will have the opportunity to participate in a post-group reflection exercise. The purpose of this reflection is to process the experiences of the group session and to understand the meaning of what transpired.

This process typically begins with the student group facilitators describing their experience leading the group. **Group facilitators:** you are expected to share the thoughts and emotions that you experienced during the group. Most importantly, you will provide a critique of your work that includes a **balanced assessment** of your strengths and areas for improvement. Then, each **participating group member**, including the joker(s), should use the "round robin" technique to provide balanced feedback for the facilitators. Lastly, the **observers** will comment on the exercise.

All members of the class (facilitators, group members, observers, and jokers) should consider the knowledge, skills and values that were demonstrated during the group exercise. In addition, feedback and reflection upon what was absent during the experience that perhaps could have assisted with group progress will make for meaningful group discussion. We hope that during this reflection exercise that you are able to consider your own skills and the skills of your colleagues in context with what you've learned thus far in your curriculum and in this course in particular.

SUMMARY, KEY CONCEPTS, AND PRINCIPLES

You've just had an opportunity to participate with your peers in a Political Action Committee (PAC) task group meeting. You were asked to consider the many ways that the knowledge, skills, and values, of group work practice and the social work profession can both help and hinder the group process. As you wrap up this experience, we encourage you to consider the any one or more of the following concepts and principles and the way they may have manifested or failed to manifest in the exercise.

Conflict theories
Systems theory
Strengths perspective
Feminist theories
Empowerment theories
Symbolic interaction theories
Systems Theory
Field Theory
Social Exchange Theory
A Model for Effective Problem Solving
(6 stage process in task groups)

Political Action Committees
The Basic Legislative Process of State
    Government
Social Work Code of Ethics
Policy Analysis, Critique and
    Framework
National Association of Social Workers:
    PACE, Legislative Agenda,
    Membership and Association
Parliamentary Procedure: Roberts Rules
    of Order

WEB RESOURCES

Center for Public Policy Priorities
http://www.cppp.org/
For more than twenty years, the Center for Public Policy Priorities (CPPP) has been a nonpartisan, non-profit 501(c)(3) policy institute committed to improving public policies and private practices to better the economic and social conditions of low- and moderate-income Texans.

National Association of Social Workers, Texas Chapter
http://www.naswtx.org/displaycommon.cfm?an=1&subarticlenbr=77
The members of the Texas Chapter of the National Association of Social Workers envision Texas as a state where the basic human needs of each individual are met, where all people are treated with dignity, where caring communities are supported, where diversity is

valued, and where social workers are involved in every facet of planning, policy, and the service delivery system.

National Association of Social Workers
http://www.socialworkers.org
The National Association of Social Workers (NASW) is the largest membership organization of professional social workers in the world, with 150,000 members. NASW works to enhance the professional growth and development of its members, to create and maintain professional standards, and to advance sound social policies.

Roberts Rules of Order
http://www.rulesonline.com/
According to *Robert's Rules of Order*, parliamentary procedure is based on the consideration of the rights:

of the majority, of the minority (especially a large minority greater than one-third), of individual members, of absentee members, of all of these groups taken together.

Parliamentary Procedure Online
http://www.parlipro.org/
Puzzled by Parlipro? Tongue-tied by motions? Perplexed by whether a motion is *debatable* or *amendable*? Who came up with the rules of parliamentary procedure anyway? With our online tutorial, here's a chance to learn a thing or two about motions and parliamentary procedure, courtesy of the public domain version of *Robert's Rules of Order Revised, Fourth Edition.*

Texas Legislature Online
http://www.capitol.state.tx.us/

CHAPTER 17

A GROUP PRACTICE EXERCISE WITH

A COMMUNITY HEALTH COALITION

HEATHER KANENBERG & STEPHEN ERICH

By the end of this exercise, you should be able to demonstrate:

- Theoretical knowledge of task group functioning.

- Theoretical knowledge of community and organizational processes.

- Knowledge of appropriate terminology for working with diverse community members and professionals.

- Knowledge of group decision making methods such as nominal group technique and Roberts Rules of Order.

- Competence in group work skills in a diverse community coalition setting.

BEFORE YOU BEGIN

The purpose of this exercise is to introduce you to group practice issues and experiences when working with community coalitions comprised of many diverse persons in many dissimilar roles. You will want to take some time before class or perhaps during class to consider the task before you. It is expected that you will have been exposed to theory specifically related to community organizing and macro practice. In addition, you are expected to be familiar with language and content appropriate for public health, children's health, and some policy discussions as well as theory and skills relevant to the facilitation of task groups. If you don't consider yourself to be prepared for this exercise and familiar with the content listed, you'll need to do some review of this essential content. Feel free to use the web resources at the end of the exercise, the initial chapters of this book, the bibliography at the end of the book, your other texts and also your instructors as resources to help you prepare.

GROUP EXERCISE:
A COMMUNITY HEALTH COALITION

You and one of your peers will co-facilitate an executive committee meeting of your regional children's health coalition (typically 45 minutes – 1 hour).

SCENARIO

The purpose of the coalition is and has always been to guarantee access to health care for all children in the region through a seamless delivery system. The membership of the coalition participates in advocacy, initiates community education and even hosts State Children's Health Insurance Program (SCHIP) and Children's Medicaid sign-up events. There are over 650 members from over 20 counties in your region of the state that participate at any given time in the meetings as well as the events and advocacy of the coalition. An average attendance at your full coalition meetings is between 50 and 75 people. **However, you are co-facilitating a meeting of the executive committee of the coalition, on which serve a total of 11 members.** The roles of executive committee members include: Chair, Vice Chair, Secretary, Treasurer, Policy Committee Chair, Provider Liaison, Outlying Counties Committee Chair, Outreach Committee Chair, 2 Members at Large, and an Immigrant and Refugee Committee Chair.

The executive committee, of which you are the facilitator, has met on several occasions and does so regularly in preparation for the quarterly meetings. There is a real sense of collegiality and the relationships among most members are strong and positive. Several of the Executive Committee members are involved with one another on other projects in the community by nature of their roles at their employing agencies. In addition, there are several community meetings (a public health workforce shortage workgroup, a health and human services advisory committee, and others) that many of the Executive Committee members attend, resulting in them seeing each other frequently.

The Executive Committee typically meets for 45-60 minutes and frequently adjourns with plans to accomplish work and finish tasks via e-mail with one another. There have been times when meetings have run longer than 2 hours, but those are typically identified in advance so that members can make arrangements in their schedules for the atypical length of the meeting. This is a **closed group**, although at times a member can send a surrogate to represent themselves if they are unable to attend. The group is open-ended (not limited to a specific number of sessions). The group consists of officers that have been longstanding in their roles as well as a couple of newly elected officers (both having attended only one executive committee meeting but several coalition meetings). All committee members are between the ages of 30 and 60. **The purpose of this Executive Committee Meeting is to plan the agenda for your upcoming quarterly coalition meeting, to discuss needed advocacy during the legislative session (the state is proposing changes to SCHIP and Medicaid eligibility criteria in an effort to reduce the budget), and to plan for and review outreach and enrollment activities for the next quarter.**

GROUP FACILITATOR TASKS

You and your co-leader are BSWs that serve as the Chair and Vice Chair of the regional Children's Health Coalition. One of you works for the local public health department in their Maternal and Child Health program and the other works at a school based health clinic in your community. **You will be facilitating the Executive Committee discussion.**

1) To begin, you and your co-leader will want to conduct some research to develop your identity and some context for this role. *See the Character Profile assignment in Group Member section.*

2) Prior to the group, you will need to develop a written agenda for your members. Jot down some ideas of what you will need to include in your agenda. If you need some assistance, you can use the sample agendas in Appendix 2 as a guide. You will need to post the agenda or distribute a copy of it to each participant on the day of the exercise. Discuss with your instructor about which is the best way to proceed.

_____
_____
_____
_____
_____
_____
_____
_____
_____

3) You will also need to prepare your explanation of the meeting structure stressing the importance of the Executive Committee to complete all the items on the agenda so that the group is prepared for the next meeting of the full coalition. This includes covering your key agenda items: planning for the quarterly meeting, discussing legislative advocacy, and reviewing outreach activities. Collaborate with your co-leader as to how to address the presentation. You may want to brainstorm some ideas in the space below.

_____
_____
_____
_____
_____
_____
_____
_____
_____
_____
_____
_____
_____
_____

4) Finally, identify, and adopt one or more decision- making method(s) to be used during the role-play.

_____

_____

_____

_____

_____

_____

_____

_____

_____

You will want to keep in mind the following points while the group is in session:

- Create an environment conducive to healthy communication and understanding.
- Introduce group members, if necessary.
- Present your written agenda to the members, checking for agreement on the proposed items.
- Prepare, and explain, the structure of the meeting.
- Use skills to foster understanding of the purpose and goals of the group.
- Use skills such as 'brainstorming', nominal group technique, and Roberts Rules of Order to facilitate task accomplishment within the group.
- Respond purposely to questions, comments, and concerns of members.
- Facilitate the group process-using available skill set.
- Develop and implement your plan for ending this group session.

ROLES FOR GROUP MEMBERS

Prior to the beginning of the group, you, with the assistance of your instructor, will get yourself "centered" if necessary, so that you may be able to engage in role playing as members of the Coalition Executive Committee that is concerned with recent threats of cuts to children's health programming as well as planning the next coalition meeting.

1) In this exercise, there are several named characters. You and your peers will take the roles of the named characters. **Before you start**: get together with the other members to choose which role you will be playing during this exercise. You will want to assume the identity and story of the member you choose prior to the group exercise. To help you become more acquainted with your role, develop a **character profile** about the person you are playing, describing the character, which agency this person represents, her/his role in that agency, and her/his role on the Executive Committee. Feel free to use the space below to jot down notes on your character, if necessary.

2) As you identify your role with your student peers, take time to consider what your position will be on the following:

- Preparing for the quarterly meeting of the full coalition (ex: guests invited, topics covered, activities planned, etc.);
- Thoughts on advocacy needed in the legislative session (ex: letter writing, legislative visits, petitions, case and/or cause advocacy, etc.);
- Ideas for outreach and enrollment activities (ex: press conference, partnering with local McDonalds for outreach to children, enrollment sights at local grocery stores and places of worship, etc.)

3) As you develop your character, we'd like to encourage you to ensure diversity is present in all its many forms within the group. As you consider who you will be and your concerns, consider whether or not you will represent an oppressed group. Think about developing a character that represents diversity in the areas of age, or race, or educational level and professional status, or perhaps along the lines of lay community worker and professionals in the field. **Please consult your instructor as you develop your character prior to the group exercise.**

Character: _____

_____

_____

_____

_____

_____

_____

_____

_____

_____

_____

_____

_____

You will also want to behave in a genuine manner while the group is in session. For instance, if you are unclear about something the facilitator(s) say, then you should express yourself honestly and seek clarity.

OBSERVER TASKS

Your role for this exercise is that of an **observer**. You have had or will have a chance to facilitate or participate in an exercise in your class, but during this group process experience you should sit quietly around the perimeter of the group. You will be assessing the performance of the group facilitators and at a later time will share your professional observations with other group exercise participants.

1) Use the following chart to help with your expectations and observations. Here are some questions to get you started: "What do you expect will take place during this group?" "Which social work knowledge, values, and skills do you expect to be present in this executive committee meeting?" "Are there concepts of group practice that you think will be particularly helpful to the facilitators as they conduct their work?"

Expectations Before the Group Session	Observations During the Group Session
Knowledge:	Knowledge:
Skills:	Skills:
Values:	Values:
Other:	Other:

REFLECTING ON THE GROUP SESSION

A critical portion of this learning exercise is the processing that takes place immediately after the exercise. At the end of the group, all students will have the opportunity to participate in a post-group reflection exercise. The purpose of this reflection is to process the experiences of the group session and to understand the meaning of what transpired.

This process typically begins with the student group facilitators describing their experience leading the group. **Group facilitators**: you are expected to share the thoughts and emotions that you experienced during the group. Most importantly, you will provide a critique of your work that includes a **balanced assessment** of your strengths and areas for improvement. Then, each **participating group member**, including the joker(s), should use the "round robin" technique to provide balanced feedback for the facilitators. Lastly, the **observers** will comment on the exercise.

All members of the class (facilitators, group members, observers, and jokers) should consider the knowledge, skills and values that were demonstrated during the group exercise. In addition, feedback and reflection upon what was absent during the experience that perhaps could have assisted with group progress will make for meaningful group discussion. We hope that during this reflection exercise you are able to consider your own skills and the skills of your colleagues in context with what you've learned thus far in your curriculum and in this course in particular.

SUMMARY, KEY CONCEPTS, AND PRINCIPLES

You have just had the unique opportunity to participate in a community health coalition executive committee meeting. The experience was hopefully interesting and added to your understanding of the complexities of group work. As you take time to reflect on the meeting and the social work knowledge, skills, and values that were manifest in the experience, you might consider any one or more of the following key concepts and principles:

Characteristics of Closed Groups
Fostering group cohesion
Facilitating group decision making
Facilitating task accomplishment

Group norms and roles
Power presence within the group
NASW Code of Ethics
Social Justice Theories

WEB RESOURCES

Center on Budget and Policy Priorities
http://cbpp.org/
The Center on Budget and Policy Priorities is one of the nation's premier policy organizations working at the federal and state levels on fiscal policy and public programs that affect low- and moderate-income families and individuals. The Center conducts research and analysis to inform public debates over proposed budget and tax policies and to help ensure that the needs of low-income families and individuals are considered in these debates. We also develop policy options to alleviate poverty.

Families USA
http://www.familiesusa.org/
Families USA is a national nonprofit, non-partisan organization dedicated to the achievement of high-quality, affordable health care for all Americans. Working at the national, state, and community levels, we have earned a national reputation as an effective voice for health care consumers for 25 years.

The Future of Children
http://www.futureofchildren.org/index.htm
The Future of Children seeks to promote effective policies and programs for children by providing policymakers, service providers, and the media with timely, objective information based on the best available research.

Health Coalition on Liability and Access
http://www.hcla.org/index.html
HCLA is a national advocacy coalition united in our strong belief that federal health liability laws are needed to bring greater fairness, timeliness and cost-effectiveness to our system of civil justice. We also believe legal reform is the best way to protect medical progress and to ensure that affordable health care is accessible to all Americans.

The Urban Institute
http://www.urban.org/health/index.cfm
A site focused on nonpartisan economic and social policy research. Includes topics on justice, economy, education, healthcare, housing, welfare, income, and retirement.

The Kaiser Family Foundation
http://www.kff.org/medicaid/index.cfm
The Kaiser Family Foundation is a non-profit, private operating foundation focusing on major health care issues facing the United States.

National Clearinghouse for Leadership Programs
http://www.nclp.umd.edu/
The National Clearinghouse for Leadership Programs, through the development of cutting edge resources, information sharing, and symposia, supports leadership development in college students by serving as a central source of professional development for leadership educators. The National Clearinghouse for Leadership Programs also works to connect leadership educators to one another and support those developing leadership programs in their communities.

CHAPTER 18

A TASK GROUP PRACTICE EXERCISE WITH

AN INTRA–AGENCY GRANT WRITING TEAM

HEATHER KANENBERG & STEPHEN ERICH

By the end of this exercise, you should be able to demonstrate:

- Theoretical knowledge of group functioning.

- Theoretical knowledge of organizational theory and behavior.

- Knowledge of terminology appropriate for working with a diverse collection of professionals.

- Knowledge of task group decision making methods (i.e. nominal group technique, Roberts Rules of Order, etc.).

- Competence related to the use of group work skills.

BEFORE YOU BEGIN

The purpose of this exercise is to introduce you to group practice issues and experiences when working with intra-agency task groups comprised of many diverse persons serving in several roles within one agency. It will be important that you take time both in and out of class to prepare for such a task.

As a bit of background to aid in your preparation: This particular group exercise assumes that you will have been exposed to essential theories related to task groups, organizational behavior and effective work within an organization. You are also expected to be familiar with language and content appropriate for grant writing and budgeting, interdisciplinary teams, gerontology, ageing needs of the Lesbian, Gay, Bisexual, Transgender, and Intersex (LGBTI) population, and governmental funding sources.   All this is assumed along with the assumption that you are familiar with skills relevant to the facilitation of task groups.

If you don't consider yourself familiar with this information or prepared for the exercise, you'll need to review some of this essential content in order to aid in your effectiveness. Feel free to use the web resources at the end of the exercise, the initial chapters of the book, the bibliography at the end of the text, your other textbooks, and also your instructor as resources to help you prepare.

GROUP EXERCISE:
AN INTRA-AGENCY GRANT WRITING TEAM

You and your colleagues have been selected to facilitate a grant writing team meeting of colleagues working in different areas of your agency/employer (typically 45 minutes – 1 hour).

SCENARIO

Delta is a large non-profit community organization that works to provide many services to the surrounding community, with a goal of improving quality of life. Delta has been in existence for 27 years and has emerged as a central partner in much of the social services offered in and around town. Through Delta there are afterschool programs, and a partnership with the local school district that results in the agency facilitating the SafeZone programming at the local junior high and high schools. In addition there are counseling and therapy services provided to at-risk youth, their parents, adults in need, and elders. The agency serves as a partner with the state children's protective services and works both with biological families to provide support services for family reunification and also works with foster and adoptive parents to provide resources and supports to meet the family's needs. Delta is well known for its work with pregnant and parenting teens. There are programs to support preventing repeat pregnancies as well as parenting courses and child care programs. Delta has worked for 12 years with the Meals on Wheels program to serve local home-bound seniors with nutrition services and some social support. From the success of the Meals on Wheels program, and by identifying the need of local seniors, Delta decided five years ago to begin a senior assistance program that would include a day center with social and educational activities that also partners with local healthcare providers that come to the center to provide needed medical, dental, and psychological services. The development and implementation of the Senior Assistance Program (SAP) has been Delta's most recent project and program expansion.

Delta has a great reputation in the community for providing good quality services. This has led to many generous individual donors in the community to donate and help fund the efforts of the agency. In addition, each year the agency receives funding from the United Way in large part because it has achieved measurable outcomes and meets the established benchmarks for quality of service. However, what many social workers and human service professionals working the community marvel at, and frankly what allows for such a wide spectrum of services to be provided, are the intra-agency grant writing teams that the Executive Director appoints to develop proposals to large local and national grant-making foundations and governmental entities. Under the stewardship of the Executive Director Dr. Lydia Hernandez, Delta has for years effectively utilized its well trained staff to develop grant proposals for new and innovative programming. This is successful, in part, because Dr. Hernandez provides the employees with the time away from their existing roles and responsibilities within Delta to contribute to the grant writing teams. She has made it her standard operating procedure to hire additional help when needed to allow for program managers and employees to "carve out time" to assist with proposal writing. She has also worked to create a culture of support for the hard work of the grant writing teams, whether the proposals are funded or rejected. The grant writing teams are appointed by Dr. Hernandez based on the request for proposal (RFP), the area of programming that is being targeted, the expertise and training of the employee, and the current workload or schedule of the employee. This results in each team having a different and unique collection of professionals from Delta, but certainly also results in some individuals working together on more than one occasion.

GROUP FACILITATOR TASKS

You and your co-facilitator are the two lead individuals on a grant writing team that is in the final stages of preparing a proposal in response to a Request For Proposals (RFP) from the National Institutes of Health (NIH) that is targeted at increasing the cultural competency of long-term care for the aging population. Dr. Hernandez and the Board of Directors for Delta have decided to expand the array of senior services and have asked the team to write a proposal to develop a special support program for LGBTI seniors that would include physical, emotional, social, and spiritual supports through the aging process. **Your team is approximately three quarters through the development of the proposal and you have only two weeks left before the grant must be submitted.** *This is a closed and time limited task group.*

You (a female) are the director of the SAP program and your co-facilitator (also a female) is one of the administrative vice presidents of Delta working with all program managers and directors. She was also instrumental in helping create the SafeZone program. The team includes: Sandy, the assistant director of the Finance Office; Jacinda, the director of the Meals on Wheels program; Charlene, the assistant program director of the SAP (who incidentally works for you); Tim, the director of Psychological Services; and Tenesha the co-director of the Adolescent Support Services and SafeZone programming. Each member of this group is valuable to the process of proposal development and writing, as they offer knowledge and expertise from areas that relate to the program Delta will be proposing. Clearly there are people with varying levels of responsibility and team members that are at different levels on the Delta organizational chart working together on this team. Your co-facilitator has worked for the agency since it opened and has worked her way up and into the Vice President (VP) position. You have been at the agency for approximately 6 years as you were hired to help request funding and plan for the SAP. You, and the VP with whom you're co-facilitating, get along well with each person on the team. There is no history of difficulties or tension that you and your co-facilitator are aware of among the members of your team.

It is understood by all of your peers that you have two weeks until the proposal is due to the NIH. Currently, there is a budget for the program/proposal that is solid and relatively close to being finalized. The physical location and logistics of the program have been all but finalized through a memorandum of understanding (MOU) with a local long-term care provider and a local hospital system. All that's left to be completed for the MOU is for your board of directors to sign the agreement at its meeting later this week. Each of the members of the team was given an assignment last week when you met to work on further enhancing the details of how the program will address the idea of cultural competency for LGBTI seniors in the areas of medical needs, emotional needs, and social and spiritual programming. No matter how you structure your meeting, it will be important to get an update from all members of the team on the work that they've done and their plans. You've asked for everyone to e-mail copies of their work for the group to review and consider prior to entering the meeting. You will need to accomplish a few things during this meeting: 1) have a check-in and get an update regarding the program budget; 2) discuss the MOU and the subsequent presentation to the Board of Directors 3) select members to help you present (the two of you are considering asking Sandy and Tenesha to join you in the presentation); and 4) discuss the updates to each area of programming that is being written into the proposal and the research to support the decisions being made. You and your co-leader (Vice Chair) have the task of facilitating this discussion.

1) To begin, you and your co-facilitator will want to conduct some research to develop your identity and some context for this role. The Facilitator is Director of SAP and is unnamed and the Co-facilitator an Administrative Vice President at Delta is also unnamed. *See the Character Profile assignment in Group Member Section.*

2) Prior to the group, you will need to develop an agenda for your group meeting. Jot down some ideas of what you will need to include in your agenda. Feel free to use the following space to develop your agenda with your co-leader. If you need some assistance, review the "Before you Begin" and "Scenario" portions of the exercise. You can also use the sample agendas in Appendix 2 as a guide. You will need to make the agenda available to your members in some way. You can post the agenda or distribute a copy of it to each participant on the day of the exercise (feel free to be creative with how this is done). Talk with your instructor about how best to proceed.

_____

_____

_____

_____

_____

_____

_____

_____

_____

_____

_____

_____

_____

_____

_____

_____

_____

_____

_____

_____

_____

_____

3) Prepare, explain, and discuss the structure of today's meeting. It is very important that the team accomplish the tasks before them, as there is a looming deadline for the proposal and a Board presentation to be done. Use the space below to outline your thoughts for the structure to the meeting. Your agenda includes accomplishing the following:

- Having a check-in and get an update regarding the program budget. Do the members have ideas of the costs of their services, staff, and portion of the program?
- Discuss the MOU and the subsequent presentation to the Board of Directors. This also means you'll need to select members to help you present, as the two of you are considering asking Sandy and Tenesha to join you in the presentation.
- Discuss the updates to each area of programming that are being written into the proposal and the research to support the decisions being made. Each of your team members was asked to e-mail this to the group before today's meeting.

You will want to keep the following points in mind while the group is in session:

- You're trying to create an environment conducive to healthy communication and understanding.
- Use skills to foster understanding of the purpose and goals of the meeting.
- Rely on your skills to facilitate task accomplishment within the group.
- You've been asked to adopt one or more decision making method(s) to be used during the role-play; attempt to follow it.
- Use care to respond purposely to questions, comments, and concerns of members.
- Develop and implement your plan for ending this group session.

ROLES FOR GROUP MEMBERS

Prior to the beginning of the group, student group members, with the assistance of the instructor, will get themselves "centered," if necessary, so that they may identify their role by selecting a member of the grant writing team and assuming their identity, role, and story. This should include identifying their role at Delta, researching the area/services they are employed in, and determining how their expertise fits in with the team both conceptually and literally.

1. As a refresher from the scenario, the following are the members of the group and the beginning of their 'story':

- Facilitator 1 is Director of SAP and has worked at the agency for 6 years. She is female and is unnamed.
- Facilitator 2 is female and an Administrative Vice President at Delta that is responsible for overseeing all program managers and directors. She has worked with the organization since it first opened, helped to develop the SafeZone program at Delta, and is also unnamed.
- Sandy is on the team and she is the assistant director of the finance office.

- Jacinda is the director of the Meals on Wheels program and is a member of the grant writing team.
- Charlene is the assistant program director of the SAP (and works Facilitator 1).
- Tim is the director of Psychological Services.
- Tenesha is the co-director of the Adolescent Support Services and responsible for all SafeZone programming.

2. Each group member will need to develop a Budget Update and an Update of Services to be written into the grant (fictional). As per the scenario, you'll need to e-mail these updates to your co-facilitators prior to the day of the group exercise. Please be sure to work with your instructor as you develop this budget. You will want to make sure that your budget numbers are compatible with those of your team members. Your Instructor will help you to be sure you're developing a rational and realistic program budget.

3. **Before you start**, get together with the other members to choose which role you will be playing during this exercise —see the roles listed above and also explained in the scenario. You will want to assume the identity and story of the member you choose prior to the group exercise. To help you become more acquainted with your role, develop a (1) **character profile** about the person you are playing, describing her/his character, and her/his role in the group.

As you develop your character, we encourage you to ensure diversity is present in all its many forms within the group. As you consider who you will be and your concerns, consider whether or not you will represent an oppressed group. There is much diversity in the team as defined already in this exercise; however you are encouraged to consider the multitude of possible other areas of diversity that you could represent in your role-play. **Please consult your instructor as you develop your character prior to the group exercise.**

Character: _____

_____

_____

_____

_____

_____

_____

_____

_____

_____

_____

_____

You will also want to behave in a genuine manner while the group is in session. For instance, if you are unclear about something the facilitator(s) say, then you should express yourself honestly and seek clarity.

OBSERVER TASKS

Your role for this exercise is that of an **observer**. You have had or will have a chance to facilitate or participate in an exercise in your class, but during this group process experience you should sit quietly around the perimeter of the group. You will be assessing the performance of the group facilitators and at a later time will share your professional observations with other group exercise participants.

1) Use the following chart to help with your expectations and observations. Here are some questions to get you started: "What do you expect will happen during this group?" "What do you expect to see the facilitators doing?" "Which social work knowledge, values, and skills do you expect to be present in this grant-writing team meeting?" "Are there concepts of group practice that you think will be particularly helpful to the facilitators as they conduct their work?"

Expectations Before the Group Session	Observations During the Group Session
Knowledge:	Knowledge:
Skills:	Skills:
Values:	Values:
Other:	Other:

REFLECTING ON THE GROUP SESSION

A critical portion of this learning exercise is the processing that takes place immediately after the exercise. At the end of the group, all students will have the opportunity to participate in a post-group reflection exercise. The purpose of this reflection is to process the experiences of the group session and to understand the meaning of what transpired.

This process typically begins with the student group facilitators describing their experience leading the group. **Group facilitators**, you are expected to share the thoughts and emotions that you experienced during the group. Most importantly, you will provide a critique of your work that includes a **balanced assessment** of your strengths and areas for improvement. Then, each **participating group member**, including the joker(s), should use the "round robin" technique to provide balanced feedback for the facilitators. Lastly, the **observers** will comment on the exercise.

All members of the class (facilitators, group members, observers, and jokers) should consider the knowledge, skills and values that were demonstrated during the group exercise. In addition, feedback and reflection upon what was absent during the experience that perhaps could have assisted with group progress will make for meaningful group discussion. We hope that during this reflection exercise you are able to consider your own skills and the skills of your colleagues in context with what you've learned thus far in your curriculum and in this course in particular.

SUMMARY, KEY CONCEPTS, AND PRINCIPLES

You have just had the unique experience of participating in a grant-writing team meeting for a non-profit organization. Hopefully this exercise was interesting and contributed to your understanding of the complexities of group work. As you take time to reflect on the session and the social work knowledge, skills, and values that were manifested in the experience, you might consider the following key concepts and principles:

Group cohesion

Group decision making

Task accomplishment

Group norms and roles

The presence of power within the group

LGBTI Aging Theories and Research

WEB RESOURCES

Center Corporation for Public Broadcasting
http://www.cpb.org/grants/grantwriting.html
The Corporation for Public Broadcasting evaluates hundreds of proposals each year for a variety of funding purposes. This publication is an easy guide to the basic elements of grant proposal writing and is offered to assist applicants to CPB and to other funding sources. It offers guideposts to help you through each stage of the process.

CSWE Gero-Ed Center
www.Gero-EdCenter.org
The CSWE Gero-Ed Center prepares social work faculty and students to meet the demographic realities of our aging society. This Web site is the online resource for social work faculty, students, and practitioners who are committed to enhancing their gerontological competence.

Geriatric Social Work Initiative

http://www.gswi.org/funding_opportunities/index.html

The Geriatric Social Work Initiative, supported by the John A. Hartford Foundation, collaborates with social work education programs to prepare needed, aging-savvy social workers and improve the care and well-being of older adults and their families.

LGBT Aging Project

http://www.lgbtagingproject.org/

The mission of the LGBT Aging Project is to ensure that lesbian, gay, bisexual and transgender elders have equal access to the life-prolonging benefits, protections, services and institutions that their heterosexual neighbors take for granted.

National Institute of Mental Health

http://www.nimh.nih.gov/research-funding/grants/grant-writing-assistance.shtml

There are no guarantees for successful funding of your application, but the following material should prove helpful as you prepare your application.

National Institute on Drug Abuse

http://grants.nih.gov/grants/grant_tips.htm

Many NIH Institutes put out guides and tip sheets on their Web sites. These guides can be useful resources. Here are just a few.

National Science Foundation

http://www.nsf.gov/pubs/2004/nsf04016/start.htm

A guide for proposal writing.

CHAPTER 19

A TASK GROUP PRACTICE EXERCISE WITH

A COMMUNITY COUNCIL IN A REFUGEE CAMP IN AN UNNAMED COUNTRY IN SOUTHERN AFRICA

SUSAN MAPP

By the end of this exercise, you should be able to demonstrate:

- An understanding of some non-Western views of mental health.

- An understanding of the impact of power differentials in international work.

- Knowledge of the impact of cultural differences on social work in an international context.

- Recognition of the difficulty of working on mental health issues in an environment where physical survival needs and safety are not well met.

- Awareness of the difficulties of running a task group in a multi-cultural context.

BEFORE YOU BEGIN

The purpose of this exercise is to introduce you to some of the difficulties inherent in working in a vastly different cultural context, as well as focusing on meeting mental health needs in an environment rife with physical health needs. This exercise is likely to challenge you because you will be asked to focus on an area that you may not know very well.. Understanding of mental health vary from culture to culture and a lack of awareness of these differences can be a barrier to effective practice. **All participants *except* the international Non-Governmental Organization (NGO) worker from the US will be given a reading prior to class explaining views of the causes of mental health problems in this area of the world (Honwana, 1998).** You will need to take time to research resources on differential understandings of mental health, international social work, and Maslow's hierarchy of needs.

GROUP EXERCISE: A COMMUNITY COUNCIL IN A REFUGEE CAMP IN AN UNNAMED COUNTRY IN SOUTHERN AFRICA

You and your co-leader (optional) will be selected to facilitate a community council meeting in a refugee camp (typically 45 minutes – 1 hour).

SCENARIO

This is a council meeting being held to discuss conditions in the refugee camp. It should be considered an open, task-centered group. The purpose of the meeting is to share information among the various groups represented and to discuss ways of helping people cope with the situation in the refugee camp, as the circumstances involving their safety and sustenance are not expected to improve. It is convened by the international Non-Governmental Organization workers who are both MSW/BSW-level social workers. They were sent here to help those in the camp deal with trauma issues, and they arrived last week. The camp has been established for three to four months. It is the first time this group has met.

In recent weeks, the supply of food and water has been running low. Yesterday, word was received that there was a raid on the supply trucks and a new supply will not be received for about a week. Thus it is likely that there will not be sufficient food or clean water to meet people's basic needs. People are afraid to leave camp to gather their own food and water for fear of attack. Rumors of a peace accord have been circulating, which would allow everyone to go home. This uncertainty of the future has kept tensions high. Not knowing how long they will be in camp has prevented the refugees from doing any long-term planning

The International NGO workers are new to the camp. They are empowered only to deal with mental health issues and have no control over issues relating to physical survival. However, since they are aware of these issues they have convened this meeting to try to work together with the community leaders. These leaders have requested that the community select its own representatives in order to empower the community to identify its own indigenous leaders.

Roles of those at the meeting: Note that there is a difference between what each individual at the meeting knows and what is said. This is to illustrate the difference between what people will share initially in this group format and what can be important to know for optimal functioning of the group. There are two international NGO workers. It was determined that co-leaders were necessary to help ensure the complex set of issues regarding cultural context are adequately addressed.

GROUP FACILITATOR TASKS

It is imperative that you as group facilitators read as many resources as possible in preparation for the meeting. This will be a task group meeting where the participants know each other but have likely never met together as a group. While there are some very specific goals, there will be no formal agenda. **It will be important for this exercise that you and your co-facilitator, once you have determined your roles, do not talk in preparation for your work together.** **You are strangers in this exercise, and it will work best as an educational experience if you only talk about what to do 5 minutes before the group is scheduled to begin.**

You will want to keep in mind all of the following points while the group is in session:

- You will need to create an environment conducive to healthy communication and understanding among diverse members.
- You'll need to ensure appropriate introductions occur among group members.
- You'll need to prepare for, explain, and discuss the structure of the meeting.
- Use your social work skills to foster trust, a sense of safety, cohesion, and understanding of the purpose and goals of the group.
- Respond purposely to questions, comments, and concerns of members.
- Have a plan for ending this group session and attempt to utilize the plan.

ROLES FOR GROUP MEMBERS

FACILITATORS:

International NGO worker –

You are a worker for an International NGO based out of the United States. You have worked with refugees in the United States and are familiar with trauma issues, but this is your first overseas assignment. Your assignment is to coordinate mental health services for the displaced persons in the camp; you have no control over meeting their physical health needs. You are uncertain how you will be received and are anxious about establishing trust within the group, especially as you are a newcomer among people who have known each other for at least several months.

You have been assigned to work with an indigenous NGO worker, but this person has little formal training and you are uncertain as to how much aid they will truly be able to offer you.

What to say initially: I am a social worker for an International NGO and have been stationed here to help those in the camp with trauma issues.

Indigenous NGO worker –

You are a social worker in the country which is affected by the conflict, although you have little formal training. Your agency has assigned you to be a liaison to the International NGO that is entering the country.. You have doubts about the benefit of formal mental health services, but will do what you are told. You know the traditional healer in this community, but also know that she does not want the international NGO workers to know that for fear they will make fun of her.

You tend to get very frustrated at the lack of respect that is shown to you by the international workers due to your lack of education.

What to say initially: I am a social worker from this community and I have been assigned to liaison with the international NGO workers.

ALL MEMBERS:

PRIOR TO THE BEGINNING of the group, you should all, with the assistance of the instructor, work to get "centered" in the exercise. You are doing this work so that you will be able to engage in role playing as members of the council.

Before you start, get together with your instructor and your peers to determine which role you will play. You will want to assume the identity and story of the member you choose prior to the group exercise. It is likely that your instructor will give you some homework to be completed prior to the day of the exercise in order to help you prepare for the experience

You will also want to function in a genuine manner while the group is in session. For instance, if you are unclear about something the facilitator(s) or other members say, then please express themselves honestly and seek clarity.

Again, please note: there is a difference between what each individual at the meeting knows and what is said. This is to illustrate the difference between what people will share initially in this group format and what can be important to know for optimal functioning of the group. There are two NGO workers (one is from abroad and one is a local person). It was determined that co-leaders were necessary to help ensure the complex set of issues in the cultural context is adequately addressed.

OBSERVER TASKS

Those of you that assume no official role in the Refugee Camp Council Meeting are going to be "**observers-only**" during the group process. You have had, or will have, a chance to facilitate or participate in an exercise in your class, but during this group process experience you should sit quietly around the perimeter of the group. You will be assessing the performance of the group facilitators and at a later time will share your professional observations with other group exercise participants.

1. Use the following chart to help with your expectations and observations. Here are some questions to get you started: "What do you expect will happen during this group?" "What do you expect to see the facilitators doing?" "Which social work knowledge, values, and skills do you expect to be present in this Camp Council Group meeting?" "Are there concepts of group practice that you think will be particularly helpful to the facilitators as they conduct their work?"

Expectations Before the Group Session	Observations During the Group Session
Knowledge:	Knowledge:
Skills:	Skills:
Values:	Values:
Other:	Other:

REFLECTING ON THE GROUP SESSION

A critical portion of this learning exercise is the processing that takes place immediately after the exercise. At the end of the group, all students will have the opportunity to participate in a post-group reflection exercise. The purpose of this reflection is to process the experiences of the group session and to understand the meaning of what transpired.

This process typically begins with the student group facilitators describing their experience leading the group. **Group facilitators**: you are expected to share the thoughts and emotions that you experienced during the group. Most importantly, you will provide a critique of your work that includes a **balanced assessment** of your strengths and areas for improvement. Then, each **participating group member**, including the joker(s), should use the "round robin" technique to provide balanced feedback for the facilitators. Lastly, the **observers** will comment on the exercise.

All members of the class (facilitators, group members, observers, and jokers) should consider the knowledge, skills and values that were demonstrated during the group exercise. In addition, feedback and reflection upon what was absent during the experience that perhaps could have assisted with group progress will make for meaningful group discussion. We hope that during this reflection exercise you are able to consider your own skills and the skills of your colleagues in context with what you've learned thus far in your curriculum and in this course in particular.

SUMMARY, KEY CONCEPTS, AND PRINCIPLES

You have just participated in a Refugee Camp Council Meeting. This was likely very different from the types of task groups within your frame of reference. While we are all very diverse and have a multitude of different experiences, many of us have not have had the privilege or opportunity to participate with international refugee groups. As you process the experience and your own preparedness for the exercise, it could be helpful to consider any one or more of the following key concepts and principles and their presence in the group:

Differential/International concepts of
   mental health
Maslow's Hierarchy of needs
Crisis, Trauma, and International
   Response to Violence
Person in Environment Perspective

Strengths Perspective
Multicultural theory
International Social Work Training and
   Constructs
Task group functioning

WEB RESOURCES

Bridging Refugee Youth and Children's Services
www.brycs.org
Provides information for social service practitioners working with refugees.

Doctors Without Borders
www.dwb.org
The English-speaking section of Médecins Sans Frontières. The information is similar to that at the Médecins Sans Frontières homepage, but each site has different information.

Forced Migration Online
www.forcedmigration.org
Forced Migration Online provides access to a variety of online resources relating to forced migration. They offer a variety of resources, including a focus on international law.

Internal Displacement Monitoring Centre
www.internal-displacement.org
The Internal Displacement Monitoring Centre is the leading international body monitoring conflict-induced internal displacement worldwide. They provide information regarding people who have been internally displaced.

International Rescue Committee
www.theirc.org
This organization works around the world to provide assistance to refugees, both in emergency situations and assisting in resettlement programs.

Médecins Sans Frontières
www.msf.org
The international body over Doctors Without Borders. Their website provides information about the country in which they work and the services they provide.

Refugee Council USA
www.refugeecouncilusa.org
The website of a coalition group of US agency concerned with refugees and asylum-seekers. It has numerous links to information for advocates of this population.

Refugees International
www.refugeesinternational.org
This organization works as an advocate for refugees both within their home countries in and receiving countries, such as the United States. They provide information concerning their projects and the situations of refugees around the globe.

United Nations High Commissioner for Refugees
www.unhcr.org
The UN agency in charge of refugee issues. Its main purpose is to lead and coordinate international action to aid refugees to help ensure their rights.

World Food Programme
www.wfp.org
This site has special pages for every one of the 77 countries where WFP works. You can find general information about the country, see its food situation, and learn what WFP is doing there.

CHAPTER 20

A TASK GROUP PRACTICE EXERCISE TO

PROMOTION AND SUPPORT OF THE PRACTICE OF PROFESSIONAL SELF-CARE IN SOCIAL WORK

SANDRA LOPEZ

By the end of this exercise, you should be able to demonstrate:

- Knowledge of group functioning through your performance within the in-class group facilitation exercise.

- An understanding of the natural consequences of helping, such as stress, burnout, compassion fatigue, and secondary traumatic stress.

- Awareness of terms, concepts, definitions and the positive and negative experiences of helping (stress, burnout, compassion fatigue, and secondary traumatic stress).

- Knowledge of the practice of professional self-care and its importance in the profession of social work.

BEFORE YOU BEGIN

The purpose of the task group you are about to participate in is to introduce you and your colleagues to the importance of the practice of professional self-care in social work through a group practice experience. It will be important that you take time both in and out of class to prepare for such a task. It is expected that you have already been exposed to theory and information related to self-care in social work, such as: stress, burnout, compassion fatigue and secondary traumatic stress prior to beginning the exercise. It is also assumed that you have a basic understanding of the importance of professional self-care in playing a critical role in becoming an effective social work practitioner and maintaining a meaningful and balanced social work practice. You and your peers are also assumed to have basic understanding of the importance of engagement, establishment of rapport, and creating a trusting environment in a group experience.

If you don't consider yourself familiar with this information or prepared for the exercise, you'll need to review some of this essential content in order to aid in your effectiveness. Feel free to use the web resources at the end of the exercise, the initial chapters of the book, the bibliography at the end of the text, your other textbooks, and also your instructor as resources to help you prepare.

GROUP EXERCISE:
PROMOTION AND SUPPORT OF THE PRACTICE
OF PROFESSIONAL SELF-CARE IN SOCIAL WORK

Two students will be selected to facilitate a task group for a portion of the class period (typically 45- 60 minutes).

SCENARIO

The purpose of this first session of the closed and time limited group is to address concerns about burnout and compassion fatigue and to develop a plan of action for responding to these conditions.   Common issues to be explored within the group include the impact of helping in social work practice in a variety of settings, self-care strategies, barriers to self-care, lack of support within the workplace, and commitment to self-care. For the purpose of this exercise, it is understood that the group is meeting for this first time to explore these issues.

GROUP FACILITATOR TASKS

You and your co-leader are social workers who have been asked to lead a task group for social workers within a social service agency, by one of the social workers currently employed at the agency.

1) To begin, you and your co-facilitator will want to conduct some research to develop your identity and some context for this role. *See the Character Profile assignment in Group Member Section.*

2) You and your co-facilitator will have the task of leading a thoughtful discussion (Brainstorming) about the following:

   • What are your thoughts about the natural consequences of helping (stress, burnout, compassion fatigue, secondary traumatic stress)?
   • What are strategies you have in place at the present time to help you survive and thrive in the profession of social work?
   • What additional self-care strategies can you identify for yourself? Can you identify possible sources of support and resources for yourself?
   • What are the potential barriers to your practice of self-care? How can you cope with these barriers when they happen?
   • What can the workplace setting do to promote the practice of self-care and to support your efforts in this process?

3) Understanding that the five key points listed in item 2 should be the focus of your group, it is likely you'll want to develop an agenda prior to the group meeting. You and your co-facilitator can use the space below to jot down some ideas of how you plan to cover the above content and what it would look like on your agenda. If you need some assistance, you can use the sample agendas in Appendix 2 as a guide. You will need to post the agenda or distribute a copy of it to each participant on the day of the exercise. Talk with your instructor about which is the best course of action.

_____

_____

_____

_____

_____

_____

_____

_____

_____

_____

_____

_____

_____

_____

_____

_____

_____

_____

_____

_____

You will want to keep in mind all or many of the following points while the group is in session:

- Create an environment conducive to healthy communication and understanding.
- Introduce group members, if necessary.
- Present your agenda to the members in some form, checking for agreement on the proposed items.
- Prepare, explain, and discuss the group rules, decision making, and structure of the meeting.
- Use skills to foster understanding of the purpose and goals of the group.
- Use skills to facilitate task accomplishment within the group.
- Respond purposely to questions, comments, and concerns of members.
- Facilitate the group process-using available skill set.
- Develop and implement your plan for ending this group session.

ROLES FOR GROUP MEMBERS

Student group members are responsible for reading the NASW policy statement on Professional Self-Care and Social Work in the 2009 edition of **Social Work Speaks.**

Prior to the beginning of the group, you, with the assistance of your instructor, will get yourself "centered," if necessary, so that you will be able to engage in role playing as members of the task group for social workers on self-care.

1) In this exercise, there are several participants but no identified roles or character descriptions for them. **Before you start**: get together with the other members to identify your role and character. Keep in mind that this is a group of social work professionals already working in the field. Be sure you consider this as you develop your character and role-play identity. To help you become more acquainted with your role, develop a **character profile** about the person you are playing.

As you develop your character, we encourage you to ensure diversity is present in all its many forms within the group. As you consider who you will be and your concerns, consider whether or not you will represent an oppressed group. Perhaps you practice an Eastern religion, or you are from a racial or ethnic background not common in your area. **Please consult your instructor as you develop your character prior to the group exercise.**

Character: _____

_____

_____

_____

_____

_____

_____

_____

_____

_____

_____

_____

You will also want to behave in a genuine manner while the group is in session. For instance, if you are unclear about something the facilitator(s) or group members say, then please, express yourself authentically and seek clarity.

OBSERVER TASKS

Your role for this exercise is that of an **observer**. You will be considered "**observers-only**" during the group process and should sit quietly around the perimeter of the group. Observers should note that you are to assess the performance of the group facilitators and at a later time you will be asked to share your professional observations with your peers.

1) Use the following chart to help with your expectations and observations. Here are some questions to get you started: "What do you expect will happen during this task group?" "What social work knowledge, values and skills do you anticipate to be particularly essential in a group such as this self-care task group?"

Expectations Before the Group Session	Observations During the Group Session
Knowledge:	Knowledge:
Skills:	Skills:
Values:	Values:
Other:	Other:

REFLECTING ON THE GROUP SESSION

A critical portion of this learning exercise is the processing that takes place immediately after the exercise. At the end of the group, all students will have the opportunity to participate in a post-group reflection exercise. The purpose of this reflection is to process the experiences of the group session and to understand the meaning of what transpired.

This process typically begins with the student group facilitators describing their experience leading the group. **Group facilitators**, you are expected to share the thoughts and emotions that you experienced during the group. Most importantly, you will provide a critique of your work that includes a **balanced assessment** of your strengths and areas for improvement. Then, each **participating group member**, including the joker(s), should use the "round robin" technique to provide balanced feedback for the facilitators. Lastly, the **observers** will comment on the exercise.

All members of the class (facilitators, group members, observers, and jokers) should consider the knowledge, skills and values that were demonstrated during the group exercise. In addition, feedback and reflection upon what was absent during the experience that perhaps could have assisted with group progress will make for meaningful group discussion. We hope

that during this reflection exercise   you are able to consider your own skills and the skills of your colleagues in context with what you've learned thus far in your curriculum and in this course in particular.

SUMMARY, KEY CONCEPTS, AND PRINCIPLES

You have just experienced task group that is focused on encouraging and facilitating self-care among social workers. You and your peers have had a chance to apply your knowledge and skills as they relate to group practices. As you process and reflect upon the experience, it might be helpful to consider any one or more of the following theories, principles and concepts were present or absent in the exercise.

Natural consequences of helping
Stress
Burnout
Compassion fatigue and secondary
    traumatic stress
Practice of professional self-care
Self-care strategies
Self-Awareness
Impact of Helping in Social Work
    (stress, burnout, compassion fatigue,
    secondary trauma)

Systems Theories
Ecological Perspective
Empowerment Theory
Feminist Theory
Queer Theory
NASW code of ethics

WEB RESOURCES

Fried Social Worker Resources
www.friedsocialworker.com
The Fried Social Worker website is devoted to issues like burnout, stress, and compassion fatigue and their impact on social workers. There is information regarding resources, tips and strategies for managing these conditions, fun products, and latest news articles.

Green Cross Academy of Traumatology
www.greencross.wildapricot.org
The Green Cross Foundation website is devoted to helping the traumatized through education, certification and deployment. The website contains informa-

tion on articles, latest research, training, certification process, and professional membership for those who work with trauma. The Green Cross Academy of Traumatology was founded by Dr. Charles Figley.

Sidran Institute
www.sidran.org
The Sidran Institute is a non-profit organization devoted to helping people who have experienced traumatic life events. There is information, publications, assessment tools, training and research for professionals and non-professionals in dealing with the after effects of trauma.

SAMPLE TREATMENT GROUP AGENDA

(Title of Group, Date of Meeting Agenda)

The goal of [name of group] is to support the healthy and appropriate functioning of its members. Together we provide support, guidance, and understanding to one another in order to help each other manage our daily challenges.

- Introductions and check-in (approx. 5 minutes)

- Questions and Issues from the past week (approx. 5 minutes)

- Group Exercise: "I appreciate you" with follow-up discussion (approx. 15 minutes)

- Discussion of new idea: Healthy Decision making (approx. 25 minutes)

    o Group leader will review key ideas

    Students: Don't forget to use your skills!

    o Group members will discuss

- Wrap up and Check out (approx. 5 minutes)

    o Closing comments by members

    o Summarization of group and introduce topic for next week.

    Students: This is a nice place to use universalizing

APPENDIX B

SAMPLE TASK GROUP AGENDA

Central State Field Educators Consortium Spring 2009 Meeting
April XX, 2009

1. Introductions and Brief Updates from Members

2. Review & Approval of Minutes

   - Need a volunteer for Minutes for this meeting

   > *Students: Item 2 could be done using Roberts Rules of Order*

3. CSWE APM & Field Summit

   - Field Summit
   - Field Director Development Institutes (FDDI)
   - Pre-Conference Session Sponsored by CSFEC

4. By-Law Review & Revision

   - Discussion of product of workgroup
   - Voting

5. Elections

   - Chair Elect
   - Nominations Committee
     - Heart of Social Work Award

6. Update on Statewide FI Training Workgroup

   - Update on workgroup efforts
   - Needs from TFEC?

7. NASW TX Session

   - Form Subcommittee to plan this
   - Paperwork due to NASW CS As Soon As Possible
   - Priority: Meeting date/time vs. Session date/time?
   - Refreshment support for student volunteers?

   > *Students: The third item under number 7 translates to a group discussion about prioritizing a meeting date over session date. You should consider what decision-making method will be used.*

8. SWRK Day at the Capital

9. International Field Affiliation Agreements

IMPORTANT DATES:
   - ✗ CSWE APM ~ November 6-9, 2009 in Centralville!
   - ✗ Social Work Day at the Legislature ~ Monday, April XX, 2009 in Center City
   - ✗ 2009 NASW Central State Annual Conference ~ October XX – XX, 2009 in Smithville

Field is the Heart of Social Work Education

Central State Voters Guide November 2009 Elections

STATEWIDE ELECTION

Candidates are listed by district, then in alphabetical order by the last name. Candidates who do not have an opponent on the ballot are listed in the guide for your information. Candidates were asked to reply within specific word limits. (Answers exceeding the word limit are abbreviated at that limit.) The Central State Voter Group has not edited any responses for grammar, spelling, or punctuation.

This guide lists responses from candidates in contested races whose constituency covers State positions for Districts 1, 2, and 3.

VOTERS GUIDE

Questions for candidates for Central State:
1. What is the role of an elected official in a district-manager form of government? (75 word limit)

2. What do you believe are the most important issues facing Central State? (75 word limit)

3. What is the role of the Central State in addressing global climate change? (75 word limit)

4. What changes would you recommend be made in the Central State Charter? (75 word limit)

CENTRAL STATE, DISTRICT 1

John Galt
1. The district-manager form of government is the system of local government that unites the strong leadership of elected officials to establish policy, pass ordinances, vote appropriations and develop an overall vision for the district. As a state official, I make major decisions and give representative power on behalf of the citizens.

2. I feel that some of the issues that face the state legislators are: transparency, homelessness, code enforcement, sustaining a high quality of life, financial challenges, encouraging new businesses, tax freezes for seniors 65 years and older, and keeping the police department and fire service as a top priority for our district citizens and repairing streets as quickly as possible, as much as we are financially able.

3. We must work to protect wildlife and to make sure that a healthy environment is present for all life. The earth is getting hotter because of the release of carbon dioxide through fossil fuels like gas and coal when burned for energy. I will lobby for cleaner cars and power plants, drive smart by keeping my engine tuned up, tires inflated helping to fuel efficiency, drive less, buy energy-efficient appliances, and replace bulbs with compact fluorescent bulbs.

4. Term limits for legislators, form youth councils, take the state legislative meetings into the community at Davis City. King Center and North Lakes, good election laws that will attract younger citizens, making sure that we represent the citizens who elected us to office and consider paying higher salaries to elected official.

Uriah Heap – No response

Mott Hoople – No Response

CENTRAL STATE, DISTRICT 2

Javier Jimenez
1. State officials are elected to represent the citizens. The elected official for District 2 should ensure that services are provided to protect the health, safety, and general welfare for all citizens; ensure effective and efficient use of tax dollars; and proactively plan for high quality sustainable growth and economic development. The District 2 representative should make decisions thoughtfully and fairly while considering the concerns of all stakeholders.

2. The most daunting job of state officials is to ensure that state services are provided efficiently to get the most out of every tax dollar. We need sustainable, quality economic development to relieve the burden on current taxpayers. Growth is inevitable, so we must ensure that our district's growth enhances its quality and livability. Codes and ordinances should be fair to all and developed through a collaborative process that involves all stakeholders.

3. It is important to think globally but act locally. We can do our part by monitoring and decreasing our carbon footprint. As we replace our current fleet of vehicles we need to buy ones with lower emission levels. We need to enhance our urban forest to help clean the air. We need to continue our efforts to purchase electricity from clean energy sources and increase promotion of energy conservation.

4. Clearly we need to have a less ambiguous wording in Article II on term limits. But as we review the charter, property codes, and ordinances we must do so in a way that is open and collaborative. The needs of all stakeholders must be considered as we work to find common ground and improve the overall quality, safety, livability, and sustainability of District 2 and Central State.

Mickey Mantle

1. The state official for District 2 sets the goals and direction for the community. Further, it sets the boundaries on the local government actions, as well as the expectations for the management of the local community. As state officials, we must be responsive to the citizens, insuring that any actions of the district are positive in nature and do not impose an unacceptable hardship, especially on the disabled, the elderly, and the low-income citizens.

2. The state is facing unprecedented fiscal issues. Sales and property tax revenues are down and will stay down; we are under-funded in primary areas, such as fire protection; and proposed legislation in D.C. will cause our operating costs (utilities, fuel, etc) to skyrocket. We are going to have to make some painful financial decisions, as we cannot count on increasing tax rates or fees at this time.

3. Any actions must be thought-out and not be knee-jerk reactions. Increased recycling, encouraging energy efficiency in our homes, better traffic flow through the district, a better use of district vehicles, all provides a high return for the costs. Actions which have little return for high costs are counter-productive. Long-term, examining the landfill for electric generation possibilities, requiring buildings to have white roofs to reflect sunlight heat, catching roof rainwater for sprinkler systems are all possibilities.

4. No response

Michelle Ruiz

1. The role of state officials is to set direction and policies for the state and district as a whole. An individual member should be a strong advocate for the residents in their district, taking concerns and issues back to the capital for resolution. A member should not micro- manage the state, but should be accessible to her/his citizens to help resolve issues that do come up. By building strong relationships with both the staff and the citizens, the member can be a strong voice for their district.

2. Given the current economic situation, the top priority should be fiscal responsibility. The district should direct the local government to work with the various departments and develop an efficiency plan for the cities in District 2. This plan should include money saving targets for each department. The District needs to re-focus its efforts when it comes to basic services, police, fire and roads, just like so many residents are being forced to refocus their spending. I will lead by example.

3. If the district can't keep up with road repairs and other basic infrastructure needs, how can they ever "change the world"? The current recycling programs are adequate for now. It is time to re-focus our efforts and taxpayers monies to addressing district infrastructure issues.

4. I think that term limits should be better defined to remove any ambiguities and loopholes. The recent controversy has created frustration and mistrust with the citizens.

CENTRAL STATE, DISTRICT 3

Hank Aaron

1. To ensure the manager fulfills the desires of constituents.

2. Most importantly, to represent the unrepresented constituency of District 3. They have had little to no voice in the state government. This includes college students, poor people, minorities.

3. The district can take many steps in stopping climate change. They did so with green cement last year. The Wal-Mart developments should be monitored for pollution levels and green supplies. University of Central State has already worked in that direction. The tax breaks for environmentally friendly home ownership is great.

4. The charter on term limits should be concisely clarified. Take away any room for interpretation and loopholes.

Amiee Moore

1. The role of a state official is to represent her/his district and the community at-large. Further, a district representative works for a healthy, productive, and sustainable community, preserving the past with an eye toward the future.

2. The most important issues facing the District 3 representative are transportation, sustainability, infrastructure, and job growth. As a member of the DCTA Citizen Action Team, I am proud that commuter rail will reach District 3 by December 2010. As your representative I will work to get bike trails and stands throughout the localities, repair our infrastructure in a timely manner, and bring green jobs to the region that will help with sustainability and job growth.

3. The district leadership must take a leading role in the effort toward a cleaner and greener community. We all benefit from cleaner air and water. We have made great strides with the GreenSense program, recycling, Keep District 3 Beautiful and other programs like green cement. Further efforts to make our community a cleaner, greener area will have my full support because our health, our children's health, and the health of our city and planet depend on it.

4. The Central State Charter should be revised to be more specific with regard to term limits and consecutive terms.

George Herman Ruth

1. The role of a state official in a district-manager form is to be a conduit for the voice of the citizens to the entire district. I believe each member should strive to maintain a positive working relationship with every other state official to efficiently facilitate the decision-making process.

2. The budget looms even larger than usual due to the economic downturn. Serious doubts about underlying assumptions of revenue projections requires cautious review and stewardship. Interpretation of the state constitution regarding term limits is an issue of immediate importance, as is deferred infrastructure maintenance, particularly streets.

3. State policy formulation and ordinance enactment must address the protection of both the natural and the man-made environments within the borders of the District 3 and beyond. While the state officials are immediately accountable to their district residents, they also have an obligation to manage/monitor our impact on the larger community for both legal and humanitarian reasons. We must be mindful to leave future generations a sustainable and livable global environment.

4. Clarification of the Central State Charter regarding term limits is required!

Hatice Safiye

1. Paramount goal and duties are to represent constituents and policy-setting and oversight for the district.

2. I think they are the same issues the district has been dealing with for the last 10 years-- which is to maintain the finest fire and police personnel; maintain our roads, libraries and parks; and coming to an agreement on the Master Plan of the Region and constantly improve the quality of life of the citizens to keep District 3 a great place to live, work, and play.

3. The state officials are responsible for promoting clean air and water, and for setting policy for enacting and enforcing ordinances that affect our community. In addition, the state sets policy for land use that furthers the quality of life of the citizens.

4. I think the charter needs to be constantly evaluated to be sure it is allowing the ctate to set policy. I think there are many issues to review.

Sam Shosha.– No response

* *This Voters Guide is based upon examples from the League of Women Voters. It can be added to or amended as is appropriate for your course. We strongly encourage you to locate a local voting guide or candidate positions statements that will be most relevant for your students. You could contact the League of Women Voters or your Statewide NASW Office.*

REFERENCES

Chapter 1: Introduction & What to Expect

Ashford, J., LeCroy, C., & Lortie, K. (2005) *Human behavior in the social environment: A multidimensional perspective* (3rd ed.). Belmont CA: Thompson.

Bales, R. (1950). *Interaction process analysis: A method for the study of small groups.* Reading MA: Addison-Wesley

Bandura, A. (1977). *Social learning theory.* Engelwood Cliffs, NJ: Prentence-Hall.

Bronfenbrenner, U. (1979). *The ecology of human development: Experiments by nature and design.* Cambridge, Mass: Harvard University Press.

Burdge, B. J. (2007). Bending gender, ending gender: Theoretical foundations for social work practice with the transgender community. *Social Work,* 52(3). 243-250.

Corey, G. (2008). *Theory and Practice of Group Counseling* (7th ed.). Belmont, CA: Thompson Brooks/Cole.

Erich, S., Tittsworth, J., & Kersten, A. S., (In press). An examination and comparison of transsexuals of Color and their White counterparts regarding personal well-being and support networks. *Journal of GLBT Family Studies.*

Friedan, B. (1975). The feminine mystique. New York, NY: Dell Publishing

Germain, C. B. (1991). Human behavior in the social environment: An ecological view. New York: Columbia University Press.

Gilligan, C. (1982). In a different voice: Psychological theory and women's development. Cambridge, MA: Harvard University Press.

Gutierrez, L., GlenMaye, L., & DeLois, K. (1995). The organizational context of empowerment practice: Implications for social work administration. *Social Work,* 40(2), 249-258.

Hill-Collins, P. (2000). Black feminist thought knowledge, consciousness, and the politics of empowerment. New York, NY: Routledge.

Hooks, B. (2000). Feminist theory from margin to center. Boston, MA : South End Press.

Kirst-Ashman, K., Grafton, H. H., (2009). *Understanding generalist practice* (5th ed.). Belmont, CA: Brooks/Cole.

Lewin, K. (1944). Resolving social conflicts and filed theory in social science. Washington, DC: American Psychological Association.

Payne, M. (1997). Modern social work theory. Basingstoke: Macmillan.

Roen, K. (2001). "Either/or" and "both/neither": Discursive tensions in transgender politics. *Journal of Women in Culture and Society,* 27(20), 501-522.

Saleebey, D. (Ed.) (2009). The strengths perspective in social work practice. Boston: Allyn & Bacon.

Toseland, R. W., Rivas, R. F. (2009). An introduction to group work practice (6th ed.) Boston, MA: Pearson Education Inc.

Ivey, A., Pederson, P., & Ivey, M. (2001). Intentional group counseling: A microskills approach. Belmont, CA: Brooks/Cole.

Chapter 2: Lesbian, Gay, Bi-sexual, Transgender Intersex, and Queer/Questioning (LGBTIQ) Adolescents "Coming Out"

Akerlund, M., & Cheung, M. (2000). Gay and lesbian identity development: Similarities and differences among African-Americans, Latin-Americans, and Asian-Americans. *Journal of Social Work Education,* 36(2) 279-292.

Besser, M., Carr, S., Cohen-Kettenis, P.T., Connolly, P., de Sutter, P., Diamond, M. et al. Atypical gender development: A review. *International Journal of Transgenderism,* (in press).

Burgess, C. (1999). Internal and external stress factors associated with the identity development of transgendered youth. *Journal of Gay & Lesbian Social Services: Issues in Practice, Policy & Research,* 10, 35-47.

Carroll, L., Gilroy, P. J., & Ryan, J. (2002). Counseling transgendered, transsexual, and gender- variant clients. *Journal of Counseling & Development,* 80, 131-140.

Cass, Vivienne C. (1984). Homosexual identity formation: Testing a theoretical model. *Journal of Sex Research,* 20(2): 143-167.

Chapman, B. E., & Brannock, J. C. (1987). Proposed model of lesbian identity development: An empirical examination. *Journal of Homosexuality,* 14(3/4), 69-80.

D'Augelli, A. R. (1994). Identity development and sexual orientation: Toward a model of lesbian, gay, and bisexual development. In Trickett, E.J., Watts, R.J., and Birman, D. (Eds.) *Human diversity:*

Perspectives on people in context. San Francisco: Jossey-Bass.

Demo, D.H., and Allen, K.R. (1996). Diversity within lesbian and gay families: Challenges and implications for family theory and research. *Journal of Social and Personal Relationships*, 13(3): 415-434.

Erich, S., Queen, N., Donnelly, S., & Tittsworth, J. (2007) Social work education: Implications for working with the transgender community. *Journal of Baccalaureate Social Work Education.*12(2), 42-52.

Erich, S., Tittsworth, J., Dykes, J., & Cabuses, C. (2008). Family relationships and their correlations with transsexual well- being. *Journal of GLBT Family Studies.*

Harrison, D. F., & Pennel, R. C. (1989). Contemporary sex roles for adolescents: New options or confusion. *Journal of Social Work and Human Sexuality*, 8(1), 27-45.

Harry Benjamin International Gender Dysphoria Association. (2001) Standards of care for gender identity disorders (Sixth Version). Author.

Herdt, G. (1989). Gay and lesbian youth: Emergent identities and cultural scenes at home and abroad. *Journal of Homosexuality*, 17(1/2), 1-41.

Icard, L. (1986). Black gay men and conflicting social identities: Sexual orientation versus racial identity. *Journal of Social Work and Human Sexuality*, 4(1/2), 83-93.

Intersex Society of America. (2004). Frequency: How common are intersex conditions? Retrieved June 22, 2004, from http://www.isna.org/drupal/node/view/91.

Lewis, Lou Ann. (1984). The coming-out process for lesbians: Integrating a stable identity. *Social Work*, 29(5): 464-469.

Mallon, G. P. (Ed.). (1999a). *Social Services with Transgendered Youth.* New York: Haworth Press.

Mallon, G. P. (Ed.). (1999b). Knowledge for practice with transgendered persons. *Journal of Gay & Lesbian Social Services*, 10, 1-18.

McCarn, S. & Fassinger, R. (1996). Revisioning sexual minority identity formation: A new model of lesbian identity and its implications for counseling and research. *Counseling Psychologist*, 24(3): 508-536.

Morrow, D., & Messinger, L. (2006). Sexual orientation and gender expression in social work practice: Working with gay, lesbian, bisexual, and transgender people. Columbia University Press: New York, NY.

Raj, R. (2002). Towards a transpositive therapeutic model: Developing clinical sensitivity and cultural competence in transsexual and transgendered clients. *International Journal of Transgenderism*, 6(2).

Savin-Williams, R. (1989a). Coming out to parents and self-esteem among gay and lesbian youths. *Journal of Homosexuality*, 18(1/2), 1-35.

Troiden, R. R. (1989). The formation of homosexual identities. *Journal of Homosexuality*, 17(1/2), 43-73.

Zucker, K. J. (2004). Gender identity development and issues. *Child and Adolescent Psychiatric Clinics of North America*, 13, 551-68, vii.

Chapter 3: School-Based Social Worker and At-Risk Adolescents

Dennison, S. (2008). Measuring the treatment outcome of short-term school-based social skills groups. *Social Work with Groups*, 31(3/4), 307-328.

Galinsky, M., Terzian, M., & Fraser, M. (2006). The art of group work practice with manualized curricula. *Social Work with Groups*, 29(1), 11-26.

Jenson, J., Dieterich, W., Rinner, J., Washington, F., & Burgoyne, K. (2006). Implementation and design issues in group-randomized prevention trials: Lessons from the youth matters public schools study. *Children & Schools*, 28(4), 207-217.

Letendre, J. (2007). Take your time and give it more: Supports and constraints to success in curricular school-based groups. *Social Work with Groups*, 30(3), 65-84.

Letendre, J., & Wayne, J. (2008). Integrating process interventions into a school-based curriculum group. *Social Work with Groups*, 31(3/4), 289-305.

Millard, T. (1990). School-based social work and family therapy. *Adolescence*, 25(98), 401.

Phillips, J., Corcoran, J., & Grossman, C. (2003). Implementing a cognitive-behavioral curriculum for adolescents with depression in the school setting. *Children & Schools*, 25(3), 147-158.

Randolph, K., & Johnson, J. (2008). School-based mentoring programs: A review of the research. *Children & Schools*, 30(3), 177-185.

Wilson, D., Gottfredson, D., & Najaka, S. (2001). School-based prevention of problem behaviors: A meta-analysis. *Journal of Quantitative Criminology*, 17(3), 247.

Winters, K., Leitten, W., Wagner, E., & Tevyaw, T. (2007). Use of brief interventions for drug abusing teenagers within a middle and high school setting. *Journal of School Health*, 77(4), 196-206.

Chapter 4: Social, Economic, and Cultural Context of African Americans Living with HIV/AIDS in the Open Community

Association for the Advancement of Social Work with Groups, Inc., (2006). *Standards for social work practice with groups.* (2nd ed). Retrieved January 16, 2009, from http://www.aaswg.org/standard-social-work-practice-with-groups

Bear, J. (2006). *Stages of Grief.* Retrieved January 16, 2009, from http://www.cancersurvivors.org/ coping/end%20term/stages.htm

Black Aids Institute. (2008). *AIDS: "A Black disease".* Retrieved January 5, 2009, from http://www.cnn.com/2008/HEALTH/conditions/07/29/black.aids.report/index.html#cnnSTCOther1

CDC. (2007). *HIV/AIDS Surveillance Report, 2005,* Vol.17, Revised Edition. Atlanta: U.S. Department of Health and Human Services, CDC: 2007: 1-46. Retrieved June 28, 2008, from http://www.cdc.gov/hivtopics/suveillance/ resources/reports/2005report/default.htm

CDC. (2007). *HIV/AIDS and African-Americans.* Retrieved on June 28, 2008, from http://www.cdc.gov/hiv/topics/aa/index.htm

Corey, G. (2008). *Theory & practice of group counseling.* (7th ed). Belmont, CA: Thomson Brooks/Cole.

Corey, G., Corey, M.S., & Callanan, P. (2007). *Issues and ethics in the helping profession.* (7th ed). Belmont, CA: Thomas Brooks Cole.

Hader, S.L., Smith, D.K., Moore, J.S., & Holmberg, S.D. (2001). HIV infection in women in the United States: Status of the millennium. *JAMA,* 285, 1186-92.

Hopps, J., & Pinderhughes, E. (1999). *Group work with overwhelmed clients.* New York: The Free Press.

Johnson, A. (2008). *Report warns of AIDS 'crisis' across the South.* Retrieved on August 1, 2008 from http://www.msnbc.msn.com/id/25819585/

Jones, A.C. (1985). Psychological functioning in Black Americans: A conceptual guide for use in psychotherapy. *Psychotherapy,* 22, 367.

Millet, G., Malebranche, D., Mason, B., & Spikes, P. (2005). Focusing "down low": bisexual black men, HIV risk and heterosexual transmission. *Journal of the National Medical Association,* 97, 525-595.

National Association of Social Workers. (1999). *Code of Ethics.* Retrieved January 23, 2007, from http://www.socialworkers.org/pubs/code/code.asp.

National Minority Aids Council. (2006). *African Americans, health disparities and HIV/AIDS: Recommendations for confronting the epidemic in black America.* Retrieved June 28, 2008 from http://www.nmac.org/public_policy/4616.cfm.

Nelson, M. (Sr. Executive Producer). (2008, July 25). *Black in America.* [Television series]. New York: CNN.

Posthuma, B.W. (2002). *Small groups in counseling and therapy: Process and Leadership.* Boston, MA: Ally& Bacon.

Prochaska, J., DiClimente, C., & Norcoss, C. (1992). *In Search of how people change. American Psychologist,* 41(4), 1102-1114.

Sue, D.W., & Sue, D. (2008). *Counseling the culturally diverse: Theory and practice,* (5th ed). Boston, MA: Wiley.

Toseland, R.W. & Rivas, R. F. (2009). *An introduction to group work practice.* (6th ed). Boston, MA: Pearson Education, Inc.

Yalom, I. (1995). *The theory and practice of group psychotherapy.* (4th ed). New York: Basic Books.

Chapter 5: Veterans with Post Traumatic Stress Disorder (PTSD)

Benda, B. B., & House, H. A. (2003). Does PTSD differ according to gender among military veterans? *Journal of Family Social Work,* 7, 15-34.

Fournier, R. R. (2002). A trauma education workshop on posttraumatic stress. *Health & Social Work,* 113-124.

Jakupcak, M., Conybeare, D., Phelps, L., Hunt, S., Holmes, H. A., & Felker, B. et al. (2007). Anger, hostility, and aggression among Iraq and Afghanistan war veterans reporting PTSD and subthreshold PTSD. *Journal of Traumatic Stress,* 20, 945-954.

Manske, J. E. (2006). Social work in the Department of Veteran Affairs: Lessons learned. *Health & Social Work,* 31, 233-238.

Mueser, K. T., Rosenberg, S. D., Xie, H., Jankowski, M. K., Bolton, E. E., & Lu, W. et al. (2008). A randomized controlled trial of cognitive-behavioral treatment for posttraumatic stress disorder in severe mental illness. *Journal of Consulting and Clinical Psychology,* 76, 259-271.

Sherwood, R. J., Shimel, H., Stolz, P., & Sherwood, D. (2003). The aging veterans: Re-Emergence of trauma issues. *Journal of Gerontological Social Work,* 40, 73-86.

Smith, M. (1999). Variations on a scream: A journey through post-traumatic stress disorder. *Journal of Social Work Practice,* 13, 29-37.

Souza, T., & Spates, C. R. (2008). Treatment of PTSD and substance abuse comorbidity. *The Behavior Analyst Today,* 9, 11-26.

VoteVet.org (2008). *CREW and VoteVet.org Expose VA Directive Barring Staff from Diagnosing Soldiers with PTSD in Order to Cut Costs*. Retrieved July 27, 2008, from http://www.votevet.org/news?id=0132

Watson, C. G., Kucala, T., Juba, M., Manifold, V., Anderson, P. E., & Anderson, D. (1991). A factor analysis of the DSM-III post-traumatic disorder criteria. *Journal of Clinical Psychology*, 47, 205-214.

Wheeler, D. P., & Bragin, M. (2007). Bringing it all back home: Social work and the challenge of returning veterans. *Health & Social Work*, 32, 297-300.

Chapter 6: Younger and Older Adolescents in a Residential Treatment

Billick, S., & Mack, A. (2005). The utility of residential treatment programs in the management of juvenile delinquency. *Adolescent Psychiatry*, 28, 95-114.

Broughton, J. (1983). The cognitive developmental theory of adolescent self and identity. In B. Lee & G. Noam (Eds.), Developmental approaches to self. New York: Plenum.

Compas, B.E. (2004) Processes of risk and resilience during adolescence: Linking contexts and individuals. In R. Lerner & L Steinberg (Eds.) *Handbook of adolescent psychology*. New York: Wiley.

Currie, E. (2003). "It's our lives they're dealing with here": Some adolescent views of residential treatment. *Journal of Drug Issues*, 33(4). 833-64.

Dryfoos, J.G., & Barkin, C. (2006). *Adolescence: Growing up in America today*. New York: Oxford University Press.

Franke, T.M. (2000). The role of attachment as a protective factor in adolescent violent behavior. *Adolescent and Family Health*, 1, 29-39.

Garbarino, J. (2001). Violent children. *Archives of Pediatrics and Adolescent Medicine*, 155,1-2.

Lewinsohn, P.M., Rohde, P., Seeley, J.R., Kline, D. N., & Gotlib, L.H. (2006). The psychosocial consequences of adolescent major depressive disorder on young adults. In T.E. Joiner, J.S. Brown & J. Kistner (Eds.). *The interpersonal, cognitive and social nature of depression*. Mahwah, NJ: Erlbaum.

Lewis, C.G. (1981). How adolescents approach decisions: Changes over grades seven to twelve and policy implications. *Child Development*, 52, 538-554.

Santrock, John W. (2008). *Adolescence* (12th ed.). New York: McGraw-Hill.

Schulenberg, J.E. (2006). Understanding the multiple contexts of adolescent risky behavior and positive development: Advances and future directions. *Applied Developmental Science*, 10, 107-113.

Sroufe, L. A. (2002). From infant attachment to promotion of adolescent autonomy. In I.G. Borkowski, S.L, Ramey, M. Bristol-Power (Eds.) *Parenting and the child's world*. Mahwah, NJ: Erlbaum.

Straus, M.B. (2007). *Adolescent girls in crisis: Intervention and hope*. New York: WW. Norton.

Youngren, V.R. (1991). Opportunity's hard knocks: Clinical training in adolescent milieu therapy. *Psychotherapy*, 28, 298-303.

Chapter 7: Single Mothers who Have Experienced Episodic Homelessness

Ashford, J.B., LeCroy, C.W., & Lortie, K.L. (2006). *Human behavior in the social environment: A multidimentional perspective*. (3rd ed.). Belmont, CA. Thomson Brooks/Cole.

Bassuk, E.L. (1993). Social and economic hardships of homeless and other poor Women. *American Journal of Orthopsychiatry*. 63(3), 340-347.

Bergmann, M.S. (1997). Termination: The Achilles heel of psychoanalytic technique. *Psychoanalytical Psychology*,14.163-174.

Brown, K., & Ziefert, M. (1990). A feminist approach to working with homeless women. *Affilia: Journal of Women of Social Work*, 5(1), 6-20.

Carroll, J., & Trull. L. (2002). Drug-dependent homeless African-American women's perspectives on life on the streets. *Journal of Ethnicity in Substance Abuse*, 1(1), 27-45.

Erikson, E. (1959). *Identity and the Life Cycle*. New York: International Universities Press.

Freund, P. & Hawkins, D. (2004). What street people reported about service access and support. *Journal of Health and Social Policy*, 18(3), 87-93.

Greene, J., Ball, K. Belcher, J., & McAlpine, C. (2003). Substance abuse, homelessness, developmental decision making, and spirituality: A women's health issue. *Journal of Social Work Practice in the Addictions*, 3(1), 39-56.

Kim, M., Calloway, M., & Campbell, L. (2004). A two-leveled community intervention model for homeless mothers with mental health or substance abuse disorders. *Journal of Community Practice*, 12(1/2), 107-122.

Kirst-Ashman, K., & Hull. G. (2006). *Understanding generalist practice*. (4th ed). Belmont: Thomson Brooks/Cole.

Lehman, E., Kass, P., Drake, C., & Nichols, S. (2007). Risk factors for the first time homelessness in low-income women. *American Journal of Orthopsychiatry*, 77(1), 20-28.

Plasse, B. (2001). A stress reduction and self-care group for homeless and addicted women, meditation, relaxation, and cognitive methods. *Social Work with Groups*, 24(3/4).

Rivera, L. (2003). Changing women and ethnographic study of homeless mothers and popular education. *Journal of Sociology and Social Welfare*, 30(2), 31-51.

Styron, T., Janoff-Bulman, R., Davidson, L. (2000). "Please ask me how I am": Experiences of family homelessness in the context of single mothers' lives. *Journal of Social Distress and the Homelessness*, 9(2), 143-165.

Toseland, R. W., Rivas, R. F. (2009). *An introduction to group work practice* (6th ed.) Boston: Pearson Education Inc.

Chapter 8: Bi-racial Children

Ambrosino, R., Heffernan, J., Shuttlesworth, G. & Ambrosino, R. (2005). *Social work and social welfare.* (5th ed.). Belmont, CA: Thomson Brooks/Cole.

Ashford, J.B., Lecroy, C.W., & Lortie, K.L. (2006). *Human behavior in the social environment: A multidimensional perspective.* (3rd ed.). Belmont, CA: Thomson Brooks/Cole.

Chang, H. (1993). *Affirming children's Roots: Cultural and linguistic diversity in early care and education.* San Francisco, CA: California Tomorrow

Chang, H. N. (1996). *Looking in, looking out: Redefining child care and early education in a diverse society.* San Francisco, CA: California Tomorrow

Cummins, L., Sevel, J., & Pedrick, L. (2006). *Social work skills demonstrated: Beginning direct practice.* (2nd ed.). Boston, MA: Pearson Education, Inc.

Derman-Sparks, L. & A.B.C. Task Force. (1989). *Antibias curriculum: Tools for empowering young children.* Washington, DC: National Association for the Education of Young Children.

McGoldrick, M., Giordano, J. & Pearce, J. (Eds.). (1996). *Ethnicity and family therapy.* New York: Guilford Press.

Pulido-Tobeassen, D., & Gonzales-Mena, J. (1999). *A place to begin: Working with parents on issues of diversity.* Sacramento, CA: California Tomorrow.

Stevens, G. (1993). *Videos for understanding diversity: A core selection and evaluation guide.* Chicago, IL: American Library Association.

Toseland, R. W., Rivas, R. F. (2009). *An introduction to group work practice* (6th ed.) Boston: Pearson Education Inc.

Chapter 9: Post – Adoption Family Group

Blacher, J. (2003). Home-by any other name-is just as sweet: Adoption of children with developmental disabilities. *The Exceptional Parent* 33(2), 36-39.

Clark, P., et. al. (2006). Integrating the older/special needs adoptive child into the family. *Journal of Marital and Family Therapy* 32(2), 181-94.

Egbert, S. C., et. al. (2004). Factors contributing to parents' preparation for special-needs adoption. *Child & Adolescent Social Work Journal* 21(6), 593-609.

Erich, S., Leung, P. (2002). The impact of previous type of abuse and sibling adoption upon adoptive families. *Child Abuse & Neglect*, 26(10), 1045-58.

Erich, S., Kanenberg, H., Case, K., Allen, T., & Bogdanos, T. (2008-In Press). An empirical analysis of factors affecting adolescent attachment in adoptive families with homosexual and straight families. *Children and Youth Services Review.*

Groze, V. (1994). Clinical and nonclinical adoptive families of special-needs children. *Families in Society*, 75, 90-104.

Meese, R. L. (2005). A few new children: Postinstitutionalized children of intercountry adoption. *The Journal of Special Education*, 39(3), 157-67.

Murphy, J., et. al. (2005). The gift of family: Murphy family with adopted Down syndrome children. *People*, 64(8), 121-126.

Schweiger, W. K., et. al. (2005). Special needs adoption: An ecological systems approach. *Family Relations*, 54(4), 512-22.

Seale-Pierce, M.Y. (2004). My road to the helping profession. *Reflections*, 10(1), 103-10.

Ward, M. (1997). Family paradigms and older-child adoption: A proposal for matching parents' strengths to children's needs. *Family Relations*, 46, 257-62.

Chapter 10: Adults with Substance Abuse Disorders

Ashenberg-Straussner, S. L. (1993). *Clinical work with substance-abusing clients.* (2nd ed.). New York: Guildford Press.

Ashford, J. B., LeCroy, C. W., & Lortie, K. L. (2006). *Human behavior in the social environment: A multidimensional perspective.* (3rd ed.). Belmont, CA: Thomson Brooks/Cole.

Ball, D. (2007). Addiction science and its genetics. *Addiction*, 103, 360-367.

Barlow, D. H. & Durand, V. M. (2005). *Abnormal psychology: An integrative approach.* (4th ed.). Belmont, CA: Thomson Learning.

Buckley, P. F. (2007). Dual diagnosis of substance abuse and severe mental illness: The scope of the problem. *Journal of Dual Diagnosis*, 3(2), 59-62.

Coombs, R. H. (2004). *Handbook of addictive disorders: Practical guide to diagnosis and treatment.* (2nd ed.). Hoboken, NJ: Wiley.

Deci, E. L. & Ryan, R. M. (2008). Facilitating optimal motivation and psychological well-being across life's domains. *Canadian Psychology*, 49(1), 14-23.

DiClemente, C. C. (2003). *Addiction and change.* New York: Guildford Press.

DuPont, R. L. (1997). *The selfish brain: Learning from addiction.* Washington, DC: American Psychiatric Press.

Elkashef, A., Biswas, J., Acri, J. B., & Vocci, F. (2007). *Biotechnology and the treatment of addictive disorders. Biodrugs*, 21(4), 259-267.

Johnson, T. P., Freels, S. A., Parsons, J. A., & Vangeest, J. B. (1997). Substance abuse and homelessness: Social selection or social adaptation? *Addiction*, 92(4), 437-445.

Gifford, E. & Humphreys, K. (2007). The psychological science of addiction. *Addiction*, 102, 352-361.

Koob, G. F. (2006). The neurobiology of addiction: a neuroadaptational view relevant for diagnosis. *Addiction*, 101(1), 23-30.

Legrand, L. N., Iacono, W. G., & McGue, M. (2005). Predicting addiction. *American Scientist*, 93, 140-147.

Miller, G. A. (2005). *Learning the language of addiction counseling.* (2nd ed.). New York: John Wiley.

Palomo, T., Archer, T. Kostrzewa, R. M., & Beninger, R. J. (2007). Comorbidity of substance abuse with other psychiatric disorders. *Neurotoxicity Research*, 12(1), 17-27.

Prinz, J. & Arkin, S. (1994). Adlerian group therapy with substance abusers. *Individual Psychology*, 50(3), 349-358.

Ryan, R. M. & Deci, E. L. (2001). On happiness and human potentials: A review of research on hedonic and eudaimonic well-being. *Annual Review of Psychology*, 52, 139-170.

Substance Abuse and Mental Health Services Administration. (2005). *Substance abuse treatment: Group therapy* (DHHS Publication No. SMA 05-3991). Rockville, MD: U.S. Government Printing Office.

Toseland, R. W., & Rivas, R. F. (2009). *An introduction to group work practice* (6th ed.) Boston: Pearson Education Inc.

Wright, S., Gournay, K., Glorney, E., & Thornicroft, G. (2002). Mental illness, substance abuse, demo-graphics, and offending: Dual diagnosis in the suburbs. *The Journal of Forensic Psychiatry*, 13(1), 35-52.

Chapter 11: Demonstrating the Use of Group Supervision

Agazarian, Y. M. (1999). Systems-centered supervision. *International Journal of Group Psychotherapy*, 49, 215-236.

American Group Psychotherapy Association (2006). *Principles of group psychotherapy.* New York: New York.

American Group Psychotherapy Association (2007). *Clinical guidelines for group psychotherapy.* New York: New York.

Bernard, Harold (2006). *Training in group psychotherapy supervision.* New York: American Group Psychotherapy Association, Inc.

Borders, L. D. & Leddick, G. R. (1987). *Handbook of counseling supervision.* Alexandria, Virginia: Association for Counselor Education and Supervision.

Brown, M. T. & Landrum-Brown, J. (1995). Counseling supervision: Cross-cultural perspectives. As in Ponterotto, J. G., Casas, J.M., Suzuki, L.A., and Alexander, C.M. *Handbook of multicultural Counseling.* Thousand Oaks, CA: Sage Publications.

Cantwell, P. & Homes, S. (1994). Social construction: a paradigm shift for systemic therapy and training. *Australian and New Zealand Journal of Family Therapy*, 15(1), 17-26.

Caspi, J. & Reid, W. (2002). *Educational supervision in social work: A task-centered model for field instruction and staff development.* New York: Columbia University Press.

Corey, G. (2004). *Theory and practice of group counseling.* Belmont, CA: Thomson Brooks/Cole.

Corey, G., Corey, M.S., Callanan, P., & Russell, J.M. (2004). *Group techniques* (3rd ed.). Pacific Grove, CA: Brooks/Cole-Thomson Learning.

Corey, M. S. & Corey, G. (2006). *Groups: Process and practice* (7th ed.). Belmont, CA: Thomson Brooks/Cole.

Emilsson, U. M. & Johnsson, E. (2007). Supervision of supervisors on developing supervision in postgraduate education. *Higher Education Research and Development*, 26(2), 163-179.

Galinsky, M. et al. (2006). The art of group work practice with manualized curricula, *Social Work with Groups*, 29(1), 11-26.

Gorski, T. (1995). *A Group leader's guide to brief strategic problem-solving group therapy.* Independence, MO: Herald House/Independence Press.

Kadushin, A. & Harkness, D. (2002). *Supervision in social work* (4th ed.). New York: University of Columbia Press.

Kaiser, T. L. (1997). *Supervisory relationships: Exploring the human element.* Pacific Grove, CA: Brooks/Cole Publishing.

Karls, J. M. & Wandrei, K. E. (1992). PIE: A new language for social work. *The Journal of Social Work,* 37(1), 80-85.

McMahon, H. G. & Fall, K. A. (2006). Adlerian group supervision: Concept, structure, and process. *The Journal of Individual Psychology,* 62(2), 126-140.

Munson, C. E. (2002). *Clinical social work supervision* (3rd ed.). New York: Haworth Press.

Northern, H. (1998). Ethical dilemmas in social work with groups. *Social Work with Groups,* 21(1/2), 5-17.

Reid, K. E. (1997). *Social work practice with groups: A clinical perspective.* (2nd edition). Pacific Grove, CA: Brooks/Cole.

Rutan, J. S. & Stone, W. N. (2007). *Psychodynamic group psychotherapy.* (4th edition). New York: Guilford.

Samara, A. (2006). Group supervision in graduate education: a process of supervision skill development and text improvement. *Higher Education Research and Development,* 25, (2) 115-129.

Schreiber, P. (1983). The use of a peer supervision group by social work clinicians. *The Clinical Supervisor,* 1, (1) 29-36.

Shulman, L. (1993). *Interactional supervision.* Washington, D.C.: NASW Press.

Storm, C.L. & Todd, T.C. (1997). *The reasonably complete systemic supervisor resource guide.* Needham Heights, MA: Allyn and Bacon.

Toseland, R. W. & Rivas, R. F. (2009). *An introduction to group work practice* (6th ed.). Boston: Pearson Education, Inc.

Yalom, I. & Leszcz, M. (2005). *The theory and practice of group psychotherapy* (5th ed.). New York: Basic Books.

Chapter 12: Hospice Planning for Loss: Children With a Parent Who Has a Terminal Illness

Baker, M. (2005). Facilitating forgiveness and peaceful closure: The therapeutic value of psychosocial intervention in end-of-life care. *Journal of Social Work in End-of-Life & Palliative Care,* 1(4), 83-95.

Benzein, E. G., & Berg, A. C. (2005). The level of and relation between hope, hopelessness and fatigue in patients and family members in palliative care, *Palliative Medicine,* 19(3), 234-240.

Christ, G. H., Raveis, V. H., Siegel, K., Karus, D., & Christ, A. E. (2005). Evaluation of a preventive intervention for bereaved children. *Journal of Social Work in End-of-Life & Palliative Care,* 1(3), 57-81.

Colon, M. (2005). Hospice and Latinos: A review of the literature. *Journal of Social Work in End-of-Life & Palliative Care,* 1(2), 27-43.

Elioff, C. (2003). Accepting hospice care: Issues for the African American community [Electronic version]. *Smith College Studies in Social Work,* 73(3), 377-384.

Falicov, C. J. (2007). Working with transnational immigrants: Expanding meanings of family,community, and culture *Family Process,* 46(2), 157-171.

Goldsmith, B., Morrison, R. S., Vanderwerker, L. C., & Prigerson, H. G. (2008). Elevated rates of prolonged grief disorder in African Americans [Electronic version]. *Death Studies,* 32(4), 352-365. Retrieved August 8, 2008 from Academic Search Complete Database.

Hope, R. M., & Hodge, D. M. (2006). Factors affecting children's adjustment to the death of a parent: The social work professional's viewpoint. *Child & Adolescent Social Work Journal,* 23 (1), 107-126.

Lindqvist, B., Schmitt, F., Santalahti, P., Romer, G., & Piha, J. (2007). Factors associated with the mental health of adolescents when a parent has cancer, *Scandinavian Journal of Psychology,* 48(4), 345-351.

Metzger, P. L., & Gray, Matt J. (2008). End-of-life communication and adjustment: Pre-loss communication as a predictor of bereavement-related outcomes. *Death Studies,* 32(4), 301-325.

Powers, D. V., Cramer, R. J., & Grubka, J. M. (2007). Spirituality, life stress, and affective well-being *Journal of Psychology & Theology,* 35(3), 235-243.

Romer, G., Saha, R., Haagen, M., Pott, M., Baldus, C., & Bergelt, C. (2007). Lessons learned in the implementation of an innovative consultation and liaison service for children of cancer patients in various hospital settings *Psycho-Oncology,* 16(2), 138-148.

Saldinger, A., Cain, A., Porterfield, K., & Lohnes, K. (2004). Facilitating attachment between school-aged children and a dying parent. *Death Studies,* 28(10), 915-940.

Saldinger, A., Porterfield, K., & Cain, A. (2004). Meeting the needs of parentally bereaved children: A framework for child-centered parenting. *Psychiatry: Interpersonal & Biological Processes*, 67(4), 331-352.

Shapiro, E. R. (2008). Whose recovery, of what? Relationships and environments promoting grief and growth. *Death Studies*, 32(1), 40-58.

Tung, T. (1990). Death, dying, and hospice: An Asian-American view. *The American Journal of Hospice & Palliative Care*, 7(5), 23-25.

Wachtel, E. F. (2001). The language of becoming: Helping children change how they think about themselves. *Family Process*, 40(4), 369-384.

Waldrop, D. P. (2007). Caregiver grief in terminal illness and bereavement: A mixed-method study. *Health & Social Work*, 32(3), 197-206.

Walters, D. A. (2008). Grief and loss: Towards an existential phenomenology of child spirituality. *International Journal of Children's Spirituality*, 13(3), 277-286.

Yarry, S. J., Stevens, E. K., & McCallum, T. J. (2007). Cultural influences on spousal caregiving. *Generations*, 31(3), 24-30.

Zalaquett, C. P., Fuerth, K. M., Stein, C., Ivey, A.E., & Ivey, M. B. (2008). Reframing the DSM-IV-TR from a multicultural/social justice perspective. *Journal of Counseling & Development*, 86(3), 364-371.

Zastrow, C. (1987). Using relaxation techniques with individuals and with groups. *Journal of Independent Social Work*, 2(1), 83-95.

Chapter 13: Couples Who Have One Partner with a Terminal Form of Cancer

Berg, C., Wiebe, D., Butner, J., Bloor, L., Bradstreet, C., Upchurch, R., et al. (2008). Collaborative coping and daily mood in couples dealing with prostate cancer. *Psychology & Aging*, 23(3), 505-516.

Blake-Mortimer, J., Koopman, C., Spiegel, D., Field, N., & Horowitz, M. (2003). Perceptions of family relationships associated with husbands' ambivalence and dependencyin anticipating losing their wives tomeastitic/recurrent breast cancer. *Journal of Loss & Trauma*, 8(2), 139-147.

BrintzenhofeSzoc, K., Smith, E., & Zabora, J. (1999). Screening to predict complicated grief in spouses of cancer patients. *Cancer Practice*, 7(5), 233-239.

Edmonds, P., Karlsen, S., Khan, S., & Addington-Hall, J. (2001). A comparison of the palliative care needs of patients dying from chronic respiratory diseases and lung cancer. *Palliative Medicine*, 15(4), 287-295.

Hahlweg, K., Revenstorf, D., Schindler, L. (1984). Effects of behavioral marital therapy on couples' communication and problem-solving skills.

Journal of Consulting and Clinical Psychology 52, 553-566.

McLean, L., Jones, J., Rydall, A., Walsh, A., Esplen, M., Zimmermann, C., et al. (2008). A couples intervention for patients facing advanced cancer and their spouse caregivers: Outcomes of a pilot study. *Psycho-Oncology*, 17(11), 1152-1156.

Rusbult, C., Buunk, B. (1993). Commitment processes in close relationships: An interdependence analysis. *Journal of Social and Personal Relationships*, 10. 175-204.

Schneider, R., Malekoff, A., Salmon, R., & Steinberg, D. (2006). Group bereavement support for spouses who are grieving the loss of a partner to cancer. *Social Work with Groups*, 29(2/3), 259-278.

Smolinski, K., & Colón, Y. (2006). Silent voices and invisible walls: Exploring end of life care with lesbians and gay men. *Journal of Psychosocial Oncology*, 24(1), 51-64.

Swensen, C., & Fuller, S. (1992). Expression of love, marriage problems, commitment, and anticipatory grief in the marriages of cancer patients. *Journal of Marriage & Family*, 54(1), 191-196.

Chapter 14: Adult Parolees

Basile, V. D. (2002). A model for developing a reentry program. *Federal Probation*, 66(3), 55-8.

Caplan, J. M. (2006). Parole system anomie: Conflicting models of casework and surveillance. *Federal Probation*, 70(3), 32-6.

Jengeleski, J., & Gordon, M. (2003). The Kintock Group, Inc.-Employment Resource Center: A two-year post-release evaluation study. *Journal of Correctional Education*, 54(1), 27-30.

Joseph, J. (ed.) (2001). Female offenders: Imprisonment and reintegration [symposium]. *Prison Journal*, 81(1), 3-132.

Leonard, M. A. (2004). Predicting completion vs. defection in a community-based reintegration program. *Journal of Offender Rehabilitation*, 40(1/2), 133-46.

Levenson, J., & Cotter, L. (2005). The effect of Megan`s Law on sex offender reintegration. *Journal of Contemporary Criminal Justice*, 21(1), 49-66.

Petersilia, J. (2001). Prisoner reentry: Public safety and reintegration challenges. *Prison Journal*, 81(3), 360-75.

Saunders, T. (2002). Staying home: Effective reintegration strategies for parolees. *The Judges' Journal*, 41(1), 34-6.

Travis, J., et. al. (2001). Reentry reconsidered: A new look at an old question. *Crime & Delinquency* 47(3), 291-313.

Zhang, S. X., et. al. (2006). Preventing parolees from returning to prison through community-based reintegration. *Crime & Delinquency* 52(4), 551-71.

Chapter 15: A Social Action Committee Addressing Neighborhood Gang Violence

Ballantine, J.H., & Spade, J.Z. (Eds.) (2008). *Schools and society: A sociological approach to education* (3rd ed.). Thousand Oaks, CA: Sage Publications, Inc.

Bartol, C.R. (1995). *Criminal behavior: A psychosocial approach* (4th ed.). New Jersey: Prentice Hall, Inc.

Clary, E.G., & Rhodes, J.E. (Eds.) (2006). *Mobilizing adults for positive youth development: Strategies for closing the gap between beliefs and behaviors.* New York: Springer Science + Business Media, Inc.

Dammers, K., Iton, A.B., Mathis, K.J., Speck, P.M., & Nahmias, D.E. (2007). Innovative tools to fight gang violence. *Medicine & Ethics*, 4(35), 118-119.

Devore, W., & Schlesinger, E.G. (1999). *Ethnic-sensitive social work practice* (5th ed.). Needham Heights, MA: Allyn & Bacon.

Grinnell, R.M., Jr., & Unrau, Y.A. (Eds.). (2008). *Social work research and evaluation: Foundations of evidence-based practice* (8th ed.). New York: Oxford University Press.

Hepworth, D.H., Rooney, R.H., & Larsen, J. (2002). *Direct social work practice: Theory and skills* (6th ed.). Pacific Grove, CA: Brooks/Cole.

Kidder, J.A. (2007). Gang deterrence and the community protection act of 2005: Why the federal response to MS-13 is flawed and how it will have an adverse impact on your state. *New England Journal on Criminal & Civil Confinement*, 33(2), 639-663.

Kingsbury, A. (2008, January 21). Dispelling the myth about gangs. *U.S. News & World Report*, 144(2), 14.

Netting, F.E., Kettner, P.M., & McMurty, S.L. (1998). *Social work macro practice* (2nd ed.). New York: Addison Wesley Longman, Inc.

Pope, C.E., & Lovell, R. (2000). Gang prevention and intervention strategies of the boys and girls clubs of America. *Free Inquiry in Creative Sociology*, 28, 91-100.

Robbins, S.P., Chatterjee, P., & Canda, E.R. (2006). *Contemporary human behavior theory: A critical perspective for social work* (2nd ed.). New York: Pearson Education, Inc.

Rodriguez, L.J. (2001). *Hearts and hands: Creating community in violent times.* New York: Seven Stories Press.

Spano, R., Freilich, J.D., & Bolland, J. (2008). Gang membership, gun carrying, and employment: Applying routine activities theory to explain violent victimization among inner city, minority youth living in extreme poverty. *Justice Quarterly*, 25(2), 381-410.

Spergel, I.A., & Grossman, S.F. (1997). The little village project: A community approach to the gang problem. *Social Work*, 42(5), 456-472.

Walji, N. (2008). Leadership: An action research approach. *AI & Society*, 23(1), 69-84.

Chapter 16: A Social Work Political Action Committee

Barker, R.L. (2003). *The Social Work Dictionary* (5th ed.). Washington, DC: NASW Press.

Boehm, A., & Staples, L. (2005). Grassroots leadership in task-oriented groups: Learning from successful leaders. *Social Work with groups*, 28 (2), 77-96.

Capuzzi, D., Gross, D.R., & Stauffer, M.D. (2006). *Introduction to Group Work* (4th ed.). Denver: Love.

Corey, G., Corey, M.S., & Haynes, R. (2006). *Groups in Action: Evolution and Challenges.* Belmont, CA: Thomson Brooks/Cole.

Haynes, K.S., & Mickelson, J.S. (2003). *Affecting change: Social workers in the political arena* (5th ed.). Boston: Allyn & Bacon.

Hick, S.F., & McNutt, J.G. (Ed.s) (2002). *Advocacy, activism, and the internet: Community organization and social policy.* Chicago: Lyceum.

Hoefer, R. (2006). *Advocacy practice for social justice.* Chicago: Lyceum.

Karger, H.J., & Stoesz, D. (2002). *American social welfare policy: A Pluralistic Approach* (4th ed.). Boston: Allyn & Bacon.

Johnson, A.K. (1994). Teaching students the task force approach: A policy-practice course. *Journal of Social Work Education*, 30(3), 336-347.

National Association of Social Workers (1999). *Code of Ethics.* Washington, DC: author.

National Association of Social Workers (1999). *NASW Advocacy.* [Online]. Available: http://www.social-workers.org/advocacy/default.asp [August 28, 2008].

Richan, W.C. (1996). *Lobbying for Social change* (2nd ed.). New York: Haworth.

Robert, H.M., III, & Evans, W.J. (Eds). (1990). *Robert's Rules of Order: Newly Revised.* Glenview, IL: Scott, Foresman and Company.

Speer, P.W., & Zippay, A. (2005). Participatory decision-making among community coalitions: An analysis of task group meetings. *Administration in Social Work*, 29 (3), 61-77.

Texas Legislative Council (2006, November 28). *Guide to Texas legislative information: How a bill becomes a law.* [Online]. Available: http://www.tlc.state.tx.us/gtli/legproc/ process.html [August 28, 2008].

Toseland, R. W., Rivas, R. F. (2009). *An introduction to group work practice* (6th ed.) Boston: Pearson Education Inc.

Chapter 17: A Community Health Coalition

Alexander, M., Zakocs, R., Earp, J., & French, E. (2006). Community coalition project directors: What makes them effective leaders? *Journal of Public Health Management & Practice*, 12(2), 201-209.

Boydell, K., & Volpe, T. (2004). A qualitative examination of the implementation of a community–academic coalition. *Journal of Community Psychology*, 32(4), 357-374.

Gabriel, R. (2000). Methodological challenges in evaluating community partnerships & coalitions: Still crazy after all these years. *Journal of Community Psychology*, 28(3), 339-352.

Hawkins, J., Pearce, C., Windle, K., Connors, M., Ireland, C., Thompson, D., et al. (2008). Creating a community coalition to address violence. *Issues in Mental Health Nursing*, 29(7), 755-765.

Humphreys, N. (1979). Competing for revenue-sharing funds: a coalition approach. *Social Work*, 24(1), 14-18.

Kimbrell, J. (2000). Coalition, partnership, and constituency building by a state public health agency: A retrospective. *Journal of Public Health Management & Practice*, 6(2), 55.

Kirst-Ashman, K., Grafton, H. H., (2009). *Generalist practice with organizations and communities* (4th ed.). Belmont, CA: Brooks/Cole.

Meenaghan, T. (1976). Clues to community power structures. *Social Work*, 21(2), 126.

Mizrahi, T., & Rosenthal, B. (2001). Complexities of coalition building: Leaders' successes, strategies, struggles, and solutions. *Social Work*, 46(1), 63-78.

Nair, M. D., & Brody, R. (2007). *Micro Practice: A Generalist Approach* (8th ed.). Wheaton, IL: Gregory Publishing Co. Inc.

Shields, J. (1992). Evaluating community organization projects: The development of an empirically based measure. *Social Work Research & Abstracts*, 28(2), 15.

Toseland, R. W., & Rivas, R. F. (2009). *An Introduction to Group Work Practice* (6th ed.) Boston: Pearson Education Inc.

Winter, M. (2004). The power of coalitions. *Human Ecology*, 31(3), 4-4.

Chapter 18: An Intra-agency Grant Writing Team

Bradley, D. B., (2001). Developing research questions through grant proposal development. *Educational Gerontology*, 27(7), 569-581.

Cahill, S. (2007). The coming GLBT senior boom. *Gay & Lesbian Review Worldwide*, 14(7). 19-21.

Crisp, C., Wayalnd, S., & Gordon, T. (2008). Older gay, lesbian, bisexual adults: Tools for age-competent and gay affirmative practice. *Journal of Gay & Lesbian Social Welfare* 20(1-2). 5-29.

de Vries, B. (2006). Home at the End of the Rainbow. *Generations*, 29(4), 64-69.

Freeman, I. C. (2005). Advocacy for Aging: Notes for the next generation. *Families in Society*, 86(3). 419-423.

Johnson, M., Jackson, N., Arnette, J., & Koffman, S. (2005). Gay and lesbian perceptions of discrimination in retirement care facilities. *Journal of Homosexuality*, 49(2), 83-102.

Harrison, J. (2005). Pink, lavender and grey: Gay, lesbian, bisexual, transgender and intersex ageing in Australian gerontology. *Gay & Lesbian Issues and Psychology Review*, 1(1).11-16. http://www. groups.psychology.org.au/Assets/Files/GLIP_Rev iew_vol1_no1%5B1%5D.pdf

Kirst-Ashman, K. K., & Hull, G. H. (2009). *Generalist practice with organizations and communities* (4th ed.). Belmont, CA: Brooks/Cole.

Masini, B., & Barrett, H. (2008). Social support as a predictor of psychological and physical well-being and lifestyle in lesbian, Gay, and Bisexual Adults Aged 50 and Over. *Journal of Gay & Lesbian Social Services*, 20(1/2), 91-110.

Thompson, E. H., (2008). Do we intend to keep this closeted? *The Gerontologist* (48). 130-132. http://gerontologist.gerontologyjournals.org/cgi/c ontent/full/48/1/130

Toseland, R. W., Rivas, R. F. (2009). *An Introduction to group work practice* (6th ed.). Boston: Pearson Education, Inc.

Chapter 19: A Community Council in a Refugee Camp in an Unnamed Country in Southern Africa

Doctors Without Borders. (2006). *Working in the field: Mental health specialists.* Retrieved October 6, 2006, from http://www.doctorswithoutborders. org/volunteer/field/mentalhealth.cfm.

Doctors Without Borders. (2005a). *Mental health.* Retrieved September 29, 2006, from http://www.doctorswithoutborders.org/news/mentalhealth.htm.

Doctors Without Borders. (2005b). *The crushing burden of rape: Sexual violence in Darfur.* Retrieved September 29, 2006, from http://www.doctorswithoutborders.org/publications/ reports/2005/sudan03.pdf.

Honwana, A. (1998). Discussion guide 4: Non-western concepts of mental health. In UNHCR. Refugee children: *Guidelines on protection and care.* Retrieved February 16, 2009, from http://earlybird.qeh.ox.ac.uk/rfgexp/pdfs/1_6.pdf

Mapp, S. C. (2007). War and conflict. In S. C. Mapp *Human rights and social justice in a global perspective: An introduction to international social work.* New York: Oxford University Press.

Machel, G. (2001). *The impact of war on children.* New York: Palgrave.

Machel, G. (1996). *The impact of armed conflict on children.* Retrieved June 24, 2005, from http://www.un.org/rights/impact.htm.

Toseland, R. W., & Rivas, R.F. (2008). *Introduction to group work practice* (6th ed). Boston: Pearson Education, Inc.

UNICEF. (2005). *The impact of conflict on women and girls in west and central Africa and the UNICEF response.* Retrieved June 30, 2006, from http://www.unicef.org/publications/index_25262.html

United Nations High Commissioner for Refugees. (2008). Global report 2007. Retrieved February 16, 209, from http://www.unhcr.org/gr07/index.html

Ward, J., & Marsh, M. (2006). *Sexual violence against women and girls in war and its aftermath: Realities, responses, and required resources.* Retrieved August 30, 2006, from http://www.unfpa.org/emergencies/symposium06/docs/finalbrusselsbriefingpaper.pdf

Chapter 20: Promotion and Support of the Practice of Self Care in Social Work

Adams, R. E., Boscarino, J. A., & Figley, C. R. (2006). Compassion fatigue and psychological distress among social workers: A validation study. *American Journal of Orthopsychiatry,* 76(1), 103-108.

Bell, H. (2003). Strengths and secondary trauma in family violence work. *Social Work,* 48(4), 513-522.

Bell, H., Kulkarni, S., & Dalton, L. (2003). Organizational prevention of vicarious trauma. Families in Society: *The Journal of Contemporary Human Services,* 84(4), 463-470.

Boscarino, J. A., Figley, C. R., & Adams, R. E. (2004). Compassion fatigue following the September 11 terrorist attacks: A study of secondary trauma among New York City social workers. *International Journal of Emergency Mental Health,* 6(2), 57-66.

Bride, B. E., Robinson, M. M., Yegidis, B., & Figley, C. R. (2003). Development and validation of the secondary traumatic stress scale. *Research on Social Work Practice,* 13(8), 1-16.

Bride, B. E. (2007). Prevalence of secondary traumatic stress among social workers. *Social Work,* 52(1), 63-70.

Cornile, T. A. & Meyers, T. W. (1999). Secondary traumatic stress among child protective service workers: Prevalence, severity and predictive factors. *Traumatology,* 5(1).

Couper, D., (2000). The impact of the sexually abused child's pain on the worker and the team. *Journal of Social Work Practice,* 14(1), 9-16.

Cunningham, M. (2003). Impact of trauma on social work clinicians: Empirical findings. *Social Work,* 48(4), 451-459.

Cunningham, M. (2004). Teaching social workers about trauma: Reducing the risks of vicarious traumatization in the classroom. *Journal of Social Work Education,* 40(2), 305-317.

Dane, B. (2000). Child welfare workers: An innovative approach for interacting with secondary trauma. *Journal of Social Work Education,* 36(1), 27-38.

Dziegielewski, S. F., Turnage, B., & Roest-Marti, S. (2004). Addressing stress with social work students: A controlled evaluation. *Journal of Social Work Education,* 40(1), 105-119.

Figley, C. R. (Ed). (1995).*Compassion fatigue: Coping with secondary traumatic stress disorder in those who treat the traumatized.* New York: Brunner/Mazel.

Figley, C. R. (2002a). Compassion fatigue: Psychotherapists' chronic lack of self-care. *Journal of Clinical Psychology,* 1433-1441.

Figley, C. R. (Ed). (2002b). *Treating compassion fatigue.* New York: Brunner-Routledge.

Gentry, J. E., Baranowsky, A. B., & Dunning, K. (1999). ARP: The accelerated recovery program (ARP) for compassion fatigue. In C.R. Figley (Ed), *Treating Compassion Fatigue.* New York: Brunner-Routledge.

Lopez, S. A. (2007). *Professional self-care & social work.* Opening keynote address - NASW Texas Chapter Sandra A. Lopez Leadership Institute, Austin, Texas, July 20, 2007.

Maslach, C. (2003). *The burnout: The cost of caring.* Cambridge, MA: Malor Book.

McCann, L.L., & Pearlman, L.A., (1990). Vicarious traumatization: A contextual model for understanding the effects of trauma on helpers. *Journal of Traumatic Stress*, 3, 131-149.

Myung-Young, U. & Harrison, D. F. (1998). Role stressors, burnout, mediators, and job satisfaction: A stress-strain-outcome model and an empirical test. *Social Work Research*, 22(2), 100-116.

NASW (2009). Professional Self-Care & Social Work in *Social Work Speaks.* Washington, DC: NASW Press.

Pearlman, L. A. (1995). Self-care for trauma therapists: Ameliorating vicarious traumatization. B. H. Stamm (Ed.) *Secondary traumatic stress: Self-care issues for clinicians, researchers, and educators,* 51-64. Lutherville, MD: Sidran Press.

Pearlman, L. A., & Saakvitne, K. W. (1995). *Trauma and the therapist: Countertransference and vicarious traumatization in psychotherapy with incest survivors.* New York: W. W. Norton.

Powell, W. E. (1994). The relationship between feelings of alienation and burnout in social work. Families in Society: *The Journal of Contemporary Human Services*, April, 229-235.

Pryce, J., Shackelford, K., & Pryce, D. (2007). *Secondary traumatic stress and the child welfare professional.* Chicago, IL: Lyceum Books.

Regehr, C., Hemsworth, D., Leslie, B, Howe, P. & Chau, S. (2004). Predictors of post traumatic distress in child welfare workers: A linear structural equation model. *OACAS Journal*, 48(4), 25-30.

Saakvitne, K.W., Pearlman, L.A., & Staff of the Traumatic Stress Institute (1996). *Transforming the pain: A workbook on vicarious traumatization.* New York: W.W. Norton.

Soderfeldt, M., Soderfeldt, B. & Warg, L. (1995). Burnout in social work. *Social Work*, 40(5), 638-646.

Stamm, B.H. (Ed) (1999). Secondary traumatic stress: *Self-care issues for clinicians, researchers and educators.* (2nd ed.). Baltimore, MD: Sidran Press.

Williams, M. B. & Sommer, J. F. (1999). Self-care and the vulnerable therapist. In Stamm, F.H. (Ed.). *Secondary traumatic stress: Self-care issues for clinicians, researchers and educators.* (2nd ed.). Baltimore, MD: Sidran Press.